101 YEARS

with

FRANK A. DOOLITTLE

a memoir

Lessons of hard work and perseverance
in the life of a local
centenarian of Bainbridge, NY.

MELANIE H. SHELDON

Freedom Way Publisher
1503 Freedom Way
Hubert, North Carolina 28539
(910)353-3840

ISBN: 978-0-6924-6062-7 (sc)
ISBN: 978-0-6924-6063-4 (hc)
ISBN: 978-1-4834-3440-7 (e)

Freedom Way Publisher rev. date: 07/13/2015

Dedication

To Frank and Wilma Doolittle, who always were
there for their family and for each other.

Contents

Acknowledgements

This book required the assistance of many others and without their help, could not have been completed. I would like to thank my husband, Charles, for his daily patience and support; David and Sharon for the interviews; Al and Pam for proofreading; Fern and Ralph for typing support; Frank's friends, neighbors and cousins for their caring love for Frank and the Lyon and Doolittle family; and to our dear Uncle Frank a huge "Thank You" for sharing his life story with us.

Preface

Shortly after my retirement as a public school teacher, I began publishing various documents. These were recollections and oral histories of several individuals in my family who had lived long and full lives. This led me to publish a family cookbook that included history, genealogy and family photos. These endeavors were all well received by family and friends.

Then as Uncle Frank Doolittle, who I consider my uncle is actually my husband's uncle, approached his 100th birthday there were pleas by various family members to interview and to write Frank's life story. Frank himself began to relish the idea of telling his life story. It was then that I decided to take on the challenge. Our family is very supportive of one another, so I knew they meant it when they said they would help me.

I have been a member of this family for over 50 years and feel it a unique privilege to tell the story of Frank and Wilma using his recollections. At 101 years of age Frank has a most wonderful memory that seems as clear as the day these things happened. The most amazing thing is, my husband, his family and I were all witness to many of these events. This memoir is an account of the experiences that Frank has accomplished in his life and is a testimony to his strong work ethic instilled in him by his parents. His dedication to family, community and business has remained steadfast throughout his life.

Introduction

This memoir is a cooperative effort by Frank's nieces, nephews and their families to present Uncle Frank's life in the personal way he has responded in various interviews. A special effort has been made to omit any personal opinions that might distract from his story. His story is mostly written in first person because the speaker is Frank Doolittle himself.

These recollections come directly from Frank Doolittle, as do many of the photographs. Various pictures were also supplied by scans from family albums of Dick and Margaret Doolittle, Ruth Doolittle Sheldon Hendrickson, and his mother Mabel Doolittle. One photo is provided to an illustrate item of the times that Frank alludes to such as his 1929 Dodge Victory six car.

Frank has had an amazing life of experiences starting with his farm chores as the oldest of four siblings, as a bar keeper and bouncer for his in-laws in Twin Rivers Inn in the late 1930s, and to being a long time President of the New Jersey-New York Club in St. Cloud, Florida.

Settle back now and travel through ten decades of time with Frank A. Doolittle and his amazing life of jobs, adventures and a dedication of always caring for others. He will introduce you to many unique personalities and friends that will become part of what we learn has shaped him and also help us understand what has made him into the person we have come to know and love. The love of his life and soul mate Wilma died in 2006 at the age of 89.

Frank will be 102 years old October 2, 2015.

Mabel with baby Frank

My Early Years

I was born October 8, 1913, in Enfield, N.Y., in Tompkins County near Ithaca, N.Y., which today is Truman State Park. In 1913 it was known as Enfield Glen. I was the oldest son of Jesse Richard Doolittle and Mabel Ette Doolittle. I lived most of my life at 5 Kirby Street, Bainbridge New York, from the year 1940 until today.

My mother Mabel was born 15 August 1882 and grew up in the Bainbridge, New York area. My father Jesse was born 6 November 1886 in North Afton but spent his early years with his parents in Lopez, Pennsylvania, at a saw mill camp.

The grandparents on my father's side were Arthur Miles Doolittle and Phebe Jane Yale known as Jennie, both of Bainbridge.

It was about 1901 when Arthur and Jennie Doolittle moved down to a lumber camp of the Jennings brothers. Today this place is a town called Lopez, Pennsylvania. There were a few company cottages, a hotel, a schoolhouse, a church and three saloons. They had their own company store and railroad to bring logs to the mill. The workers who had families lived in the cottages owned by the company.

My grandfather Arthur went about cutting timber, while my grandmother, Jennie, worked in the hotel. The family actually lived in the hotel. My father Jesse was about fifteen years old at that time and worked at the sawmill with his father.

Up above this lumber town was a coal mine. My father used to tell the story that he and about fifteen others decided that they didn't want to work at the mill anymore. So they went up to the coal mine and were hired to drive the mules that pulled the coal cars up out of the mine.

My father became friends with an old Irishman down in the mine. He had a spot carved out in the sidewall where he kept his tools and stayed in this little room. He took the boys under his wing and helped them. After some time passed there was a cave-in and the Irishman was killed in his room. That was the end of their mining. Jesse and the others didn't want to be down in there anymore.

The Jennings brothers moved to up-state NY in the Buffalo area when they finished the timber and lumbering in Pennsylvania. That's when my grandparents moved back to Bainbridge. Some of the people who lived in the cottages bought them from the company and stayed there in Lopez.

note: the Jennings brothers built factories to convert wastage into such products as kindling wood, clothes pins, broom handles, baseball bats, staves, washboards, matches and many other articles, many of which have been replaced today with plastics. The Jennings mill factories, railroad and logging operations in 1900 provided employment for 600 men and gave Lopez a population of 1200. Natural streams powered mills were used for sawing lumber and for grinding grain. Saw mills outnumbered gristmills in the nation 10 to 1. Many towns were built around a sawmill, which has a primitive water wheel that powered the mill. The saw itself was an up-and-down saw, which cut approximately 1000 feet of lumber in 10 hours of work each day. This may have been the place and era of when 15 year old Jesse Doolittle developed a desire to saw lumber and to make handles for his own business in later years in Bainbridge, New York.[1]

My grandparents on my mother's side were Andress Darling Doolittle and Cora Belle Davis, both of Bainbridge.

My mother's folks had a farm in Bainbridge, when her mother Cora's relatives got sick. Many people in the community were suffering with typhoid fever at the time. My grandmother went to take care of her nephews at her brother Menzo Davis' home near Brackett Lake and got sick herself. She was unable to come home because typhoid fever was very contagious. She died of the dread disease in 1902 as well as her brother Menzo a year earlier. She was only 40 years old.

So my mother was left to care for her three brothers, Perry, Mark and Floyd Doolittle. Sometime after that, around 1905 her father Andress left the farm while her oldest brother Perry was still living at home.

---

[1] www.rootsweb.ancestry.com/pasulliv/SullivanCountyHistoricalSociety/
Sullivanindustries.htm

Andress Doolittle, grandfather on my mother's side.

Andress Doolittle, my grandfather, married again. He married Maude Wykes in 1906, and they lived upstairs in the same house as my father's parents, Arthur and Jennie Doolittle. Andress and Maude had a son in 1925 named John Elliot Doolittle Hurlburt.

Later, my mother attended Oxford Teachers Academy for training to become a teacher and began to teach soon in the following schools of the Pond District:

West Bainbridge, Brackett Lake, and Guilford Center. She rode the stage to a schoolhouse on the road to Deposit and she lived in a farmhouse up on a hill while she taught school there. Friday night she'd ride with the mail carrier to come home to Bainbridge. It was during this time of weekend visits that my father Jesse came to town and they met for the first time. They ended up marrying in 1912. They were actually first cousins because their fathers were brothers.

Jesse and Mabel Doolittle's first house 1913 where I was born.

Their first home was in Enfield where they lived from 1912 until 1916. We were living there when my brother Paul and I were both born.

In those days, she always used a horse and sulky or wagon for travel. A sulky was a light 2-wheeled horse drawn cart with only a seat for the driver. She used a brown mare, an older horse, even after she married, in Enfield.

Horses were an important way of travel as well as for work on the farm. Road 206 was a single lane dirt road. Horses hauled everything in those days. Our favorite horse was "Old Jim", a white horse. "Old Jim" was used to cultivate crops and to pull wagons and carts.

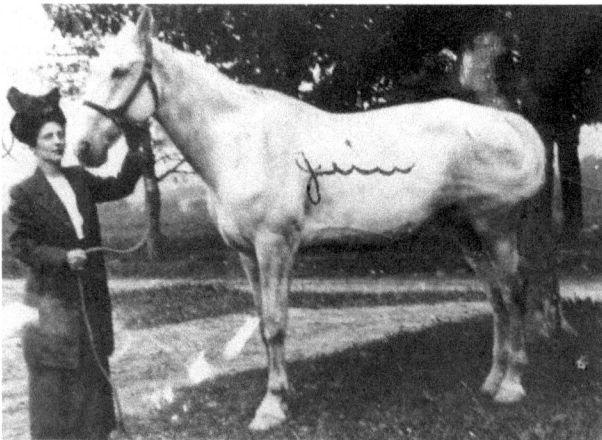

Mabel and "Old Jim" our favorite horse. 1914

We had a horse that had been a racehorse and had quite a record in racing. But suddenly decided he wouldn't go all the way around the track anymore while racing. He would go just so far, turn around, and go back.

My grandfather Arthur would come to visit us in Enfield. My grandmother wouldn't ride with him because she said, "He went so like the wind." She just knew he was going to get killed. He made many trips to Enfield on all dirt roads. There was a tavern over in the triangle, half way between Bainbridge and Enfield. He had to stop to rest the horse. It was a two-day trip he'd make in one day. This horse only had one gait, uphill and down. He didn't know how to walk.

Over the years I've seen many pictures of me. There's one of me playing with a neighbor boy when I was 5 years old but I don't remember getting my picture taken. There were many times my father would take me hunting with him to get meat for the table, and I went on many trips with him.

My grandmother Jennie went to the Baptist Church in West Bainbridge. It was on an old road that was the same level as the church. There was a hole beneath the bridge they used for baptisms. Whenever my grandfather Arthur went that way, he had to go down through that hole instead of over the bridge. He said he had to soak up his buggy wheel so it wouldn't rattle. Grandma didn't think that was right. Said he was an "old heathen." I don't remember him ever going to church.

My grandmother Phebe Jane "Jennie", on the other hand, played the organ, and had lots of church music in their living room. She was active in the church. On one side of the living room were her church papers and music, and on the other side were grandfather's Red Book magazines and things he read.

One time grandmother packed up all her dishes and went to Binghamton to stay with my father's sister up there. She lived there for a while and grandfather had to use his own dishes while she was gone.

Grandma Jennie Doolittle in her chair reading.

We moved from Enfield to a farm known as the Eastman farm on route 206, West Bainbridge in 1916. This house had a wrap around porch and was up on a hill. It had a wood shed in the back. One of my chores was to get wood out of the shed and bring it in to the kitchen for the wood-burning stove. There were about 7 rooms, 3 bedrooms, a kitchen and a long hall that went through the woodshed to our outhouse. So we didn't have to go outside to the outhouse. The big kitchen had a large table and had enough room for our family. There were at least 3 rooms upstairs used as bedrooms. We had a cellar under the house. Down the hill below the house was a store place that was part granary and part corn crib.

The grain was for the animals. Part of this granary was on stilts where my father kept his trained hunting dogs under part of it. He trained dogs up in Enfield, too, for other people. Down further was a flat where the big barn was and a stable with a lean-to built on it for the horses.

In Union Valley there was the Unadilla Methodist Church. I was a member of this church along with my family. My father went to church sometimes. When my father got a car, he decided to go to Bainbridge to church. I'm pretty sure Hudson Lyon persuaded him to attend the Presbyterian Church. In the winters, there had to be some kind of shelter for the horses when they came into town, keeping them out of the bad weather. Hudson had a church shed that he didn't use so he gave it to my father. Then we went to Bainbridge to the Presbyterian Church.

When we lived on the Eastman farm, they formed a group in Union Valley that had a Community House. Father was one of the directors. When people came to the meetings, members would put their horses in the shed at the Methodist Church.

Doolittle family group at Eastman farm. Standing L to R: Floyd, Jesse holding Ruth, Mark and Perry Doolittle. Seated: Arthur holding Richard, Jennie (Arthur's wife), Mary Doolittle holding Leland, Andress Doolittle. Those seated below are Frank, Andy, Joe, Marie (Floyd's wife) and Ellen.

On one very cold night when father used "Old Jim" to pick up folks at night for a community meeting, and let them all out in front of the building. He tied the horse and cart containing all the fur coats in the shed. "Old Jim" got untied and tipped the cart and dumped all the fur coats on the ground and then went home to the barn and waited. Everyone had to walk home, which was about 3 miles in the bad weather. Dad was somewhat embarrassed and upset with "Old Jim."

My dad became active in the church and attended the men's class in Sunday school and was a Trustee. He became a town councilman and joined the Masonic Lodge and the Rotary Club. He was more active in the Rotary Club because it met during the daytime. He liked to hunt and fish but mostly stayed around home.

One fall there was a group of men who'd wanted him to go hunting deer up north. He went along and they stationed him close to camp with a small rifle. A guide told him he had a "bee shooter." He waited there most of the day, and when a deer came, he shot it. It was the only deer they got that trip.

My mother's uncle had a general store in the house across from the church. Uncle Melvin Herrick lived in the big family house at the crossroads. He married Adelia Davis of Union Valley.

Up above there, the Hawleys ran another store and towards Herrick's place, was another. There were 3 stores in Union Valley at that time.

I remember one time my father went to Bainbridge to his mother's (Jennie) place to have surgery. Dr. Danforth performed the surgery. My father had to stay there for a time to recover. While he was there Uncle Will Davis (mother's brother) came to our house to do chores and other work on the farm. It was wintertime and in the daytime the cows went into the creek (Kelsey Brook) to get a drink.

While Uncle Will cleaned the stable one-day, I was at the farm to help him. Being only five years old at the time, I followed the cows on the flats to the creek. About half way there was a spring where some of the cows drank. It was icy there and I slid into the spring. Uncle Will happened to see me and ran down there to fish me out. I had a new pair of boots on and lost one boot in the spring and was put out because Uncle Will wouldn't find it.

The Silvernails were friends of our family who lived in the next place up in West Bainbridge. She was a Sunday school teacher. They killed a cow once that came after me when I was small. The cow looked straight at me and started towards me so I ran to the fence to get away. But the cow got to me and smashed me against the fence before I could get there. My father saw what happened and came over. He looked for a large stone to hit the cow, but couldn't find one so started smashing the cow with his fists. It messed his hands up so that he couldn't milk cows. The Silvernails decided to kill the cow the next day.

Then there was the morning Uncle Will came in for breakfast, and Ma didn't have it ready yet because she was trying to get my little brother dressed. Uncle Will said, "Give me that young one and I'll dress him." Needless to say, that from then on Paul was dressed and breakfast was ready when Uncle Will came in.

One day while we still lived there, Ma had gone to pick blueberries in a field on the other side of the farm and left me to look after my two brothers. The preacher came to call and thought I had to entertain him so I asked him if he wanted to go down to the cellar to get a drink of beer. Ma made root beer in the summer and left it in the cellar to keep it cool. I do not remember this but was told about it later.

We moved from this farm in November 1919 to the farm where we grew up and where Richard Doolittle still lives. It was commonly called the "Pine Stock Farm" and was on Lyon Road, just outside of Bainbridge. The Lyon family of 4 pioneer brothers originally settled this farm in West Bainbridge in 1803. Hudson Lyon was the grandson of one of these brothers, Charles Lyon, so Hudson inherited this farm. My parents bought the farm from Hudson Lyon.

After my folks moved to the Lyon farm, dad's parents moved to the farm to help out. They lived in part of the house. I referred to him as "Big Grandfather," mainly because he was taller than my other grandfather, Andress.

Grandfather Arthur had one horse to cultivate crops. He had me ride the horse to guide it while he cultivated. Grandfather helped us out a lot, helping with the chores and gardening.

I remember there was an election around 1928, and my grandparents Arthur and Jennie had big posters in the windows of the house promoting their candidates. Her poster was in the front window that faced the road; that was supporting Al Smith, Democrat. Grandfather had his poster of Herbert Hoover, Republican in the other window, on the side. There was quite a bit of difference of opinion in our house when it came to politics.

My grandfather Arthur died in 1927, and my grandmother Jennie died in 1930 at her daughter's Anna Transue home in Binghamton. Grandma was Phebe Jane Yale but everyone knew her as Jennie.

My mother was really good at keeping books, and running things. For a few years we made maple products on the farm with an evaporator. We tapped around 500 trees, most trees having 3-4 buckets. We made maple syrup and maple butter using various forms to make sugar cakes, stars and hearts. We also had a bigger square cake form that was used to make a pound of maple sugar. The best place for us to make the sugar was out in the edge of the woods. Then we brought the syrup to the house where we cooked it down and canned it in gallon tins and put maple butter in five-pound tin pails. Twice I had to tend sap boiling all night. It had to be kept hot but not burn. The finishing pan was the one hardest to watch because it was thick by this time. That went on for several years providing extra income while my mother kept the books for the farm.

Considering there were four of us children, sometimes we had to be disciplined. It was my mother who usually did the discipline. She used whips from the lilac bush or if late in the day, to stand up while eating supper. My father was about the size of his father, a bigger man than me. When we'd get noisy, he'd discipline us sometimes by saying, "Hark that noise before I thump you!" and we knew what that meant, and settled down.

Frank at 2 years of age.

As young children we liked to play in mud puddles. I can remember there was a washtub in the back yard with cold water. We'd take off our clothes and get washed off out there, and then go to bed.

My mother wanted to live on the farm so that's where we lived. But I don't think my father was a farmer. He ran the farms until about 1928. That's when he got a job working for the Union Handle Company buying ash logs for the mill in Frankfort, NY. Of course, he was away a lot but would be home on the weekends. We had a dairy, and I was the one who took care of the dairy and saw that the all the work got done. This was while I was still going to school.

We had some Rhode Island Red chickens on the farm and chicken was my favorite meat. My mother made biscuits and gravy, and rolls, and the best roast chicken I ever had. She canned blueberries and blackberries in the summer time and put them in the cellar. She canned a lot of food from the farm and stored for the winter. Her canned tomatoes, string beans, corn, beets and cucumber pickles were delicious to eat throughout the cold winter months.

The farmers stuck together in those days. Our farm never had a silo, but my father got a corn harvester and went around cutting corn at different places. I remember driving the harvester. We had one 2-horse team and a 3-horse team. Whenever we cut corn, the other farmer would supply a horse for the team. There was one farm where I went; the farmer supplied a mule for the team. We didn't know how that would work because we liked to use horses. We always put the spare horse in the middle. But they worked out well, even though they had never seen one another before. The mule pulled his share and they got the corn cut.

No money exchanged hands; the farmers just helped one another in those days. One farmer owned the threshing machine and the gas engine that ran it, and another one had a silage blower to fill silos. That's the way they worked. One farmer didn't need all the equipment. Our own corn was cut and chopped in the field, because we didn't have a silo to store the corn.

In cold weather, we'd bring in what we had room for on the barn floor. We'd pick the ears off, husk them and put them in the granaries. The stalks and shucks were chopped and blown by the machine into an area for animal feed. We had a corn sheller to put whole corn in with oats and hay for the horses. The pigs were given whole corn and the cobs. Also, the chickens ate some of the corn. There was always enough for all the livestock.

When I think back over the years, I don't know how my folks managed to get along as well as they did with not much money, a mortgage on the farm and health expenses. I've always wondered how they managed to feed us as they did. Most of our food was raised there on the farm, and I feel we lived better than most of the town kids. We didn't think we did at the time. There wasn't much money to use at all.

Arthur, Jesse and young Frank, a 3-generation picture.

1920 picture of the Doolittle farm on Lyon Road

School and Farming Years

When we moved to the farm on Lyon Road, I was six years old. It was a dairy farm and I had chores. I got up at 5:00 in the morning to get out to the barn and do my chores. I got an allowance of seventy-five cents a week. Any little job someone could have would be paid twenty-five cents. I spent my money wisely and saved some.

The first two years our parents had to make sure we got to Bainbridge for school. We all had to meet at the old schoolhouse to get a ride from there to the Bainbridge school. I went to the Bainbridge Union School (picture) until it was torn down in 1926. The new school was built in the same place as the old one.

My mother taught me at home how to write my name and to read some before I started first grade in Bainbridge. It was a long day because the school hours were from 9 to 4, all day starting with first grade.

When I started school my teacher was Miss Dotsie. Mr. Casey came that year, and he was principal of Bainbridge Central K-12 for many years. Then the next year Anna Nailer was my teacher.

There is one incident I will always remember. In third grade there was an Italian girl sitting in front of me. She had long dark hair and the top was off my ink well. Her hair began to swish around in the black ink and got all over her clothes. She let out a loud "war whoop," and the teacher came to see what was wrong. It was entirely my fault, she said.

The teacher took me to her desk, and with her meter stick, said, "Hold your hand out and bend your fingers back." The stick broke when she wacked me, and part of it went right up to the ceiling and came down on the row next to me. It landed on a friend's desk next to me, and I began to laugh and others laughed, too. She made me go out into the hall, where there was a dark area for me to sit.

Bainbridge Union School 1920

The sixth and seventh grades were in the old cigar factory because the old 1874 school had been torn down in 1926. Other classes were meeting all around town while the new school was being built.

Two of my teachers stand out: Mildred Patley and Eloise Williams (married Charlie Hager). After getting into high school, I was signed up for Ancient History with Eloise Williams, and English with Mildred Parley at the same time by mistake. They asked if I wanted to change my schedule, but I kept it as it was. I was able to keep my grades up to passing in both classes.

The Ag Class in 1932 Echo Yearbook of Bainbridge Central,
Frank 2nd row next to the last, Mr. Coe teacher front center.

My favorite class was Agriculture with Oris Coe. That year I joined the Future Farmers of America. This is when there came an opportunity for me to go around to the dairy farms in the area and to keep records for the dairy farmers.

There was a controversy between some of the dairy farmers and the milk plants in the community. The farmers thought they were being cheated. They heard talk that some dairy farmers were getting more for their milk. So I weighed the cows, tested the milk, and kept good records. This took a lot of time after school for me, but at the time we didn't have a dairy at home. The Holstein cow's milk was low in butterfat, and a lot of the farmers had Holsteins. The amount of butterfat in the milk affected the price they received from the plant. This helped settle the controversy between the farmers and the milk company when they saw my records.

Jesse checking a Holstein cow on his farm.

Hudson Lyon who owned the dairy farm before our family, wrote articles for various local newspapers and to agricultural journals. He wanted me to do some research on his dairy in order to put it in his papers. So I did and then he wanted to repay me for the work I'd done on his cows. There was a Farm and Home Week at Cornell University, and he invited me to go with him. We went on a Flier Train to a house where Hudson stayed that had several rooms. The next day we went over to the campus to attend some lectures and to get some information for his writing. We stayed there three days. The last day we went to the library. I was very interested in the bells in the tower. There was a stairway to the bells and I was shown inside where a man played the big bells. Then I went down and Hudson said, "They used to have bells here, I don't know why they don't play anymore" He was almost completely deaf and couldn't hear them ringing.

During the year before, there had been a diphtheria epidemic in our town and many people had died. Some of us students were identified as carriers of the disease. They put us out in the old barn for classes. All the grades were there with one teacher. Mr. Casey would bring the lessons over to us. We basically lost that year, about 1928, by playing games all day. The clock in the barn was covered in spitballs at the end of the year. I was a member of the Class of 1932 but could not graduate until 1933 because of lack of studies that year.

One year during New York Regents testing, I had to take the Algebra Regents Test. We started and I went through and answered everything and took it up to the teacher. It was easy and I had finished it first. She said, "Oh, no, you need to take it back and read through more carefully and answer everything." So I took it back, looked out the window and waited until it was time to hand it in. That night the teacher called my mother to talk about the test. She told my mother that I had made a 95, which was really good she said.

When I was probably 13 or so, my grandfather Arthur had always hauled our milk to Bainbridge. He got so he couldn't do it any more so I took the milk when I went to school and left the rig at the livery stable.

Thanksgiving day at "the Pines"
1920

Doolittle farm 1920 snow.

In the winter of 1925 or 1926 usually on Friday night, Gibby Howland used to ride the rig up to the corner of his grandfather's farm; that's where

Smiths live now. He is the son-in-law of Doc Benson. That was Howland's place at that time. The grandfather had the farm, and the Howlands had a grocery store in Bainbridge. His son was Gibby Howland. Those days had harsh winters so sleighing was maybe three months or so. In those days we had a rig that was a sleigh to get to school.

Later on the man that took us to school lived up across the road from Haddads. Malcolm Ray lived there and he took us so we just had to walk to his house. They had a dairy farm and made butter and peddled it around town. One day he came to town peddling his butter and stopped out there where the body shop is now. That was the feed store (GLF). He stopped there with some of his butter, and while he was in there a train came through and something spooked his horses. They started to run and got on the track ahead of the train, and, of course, it killed the horses and cracked the sleigh.

They had to get somebody else to take us to school. So they got Andrew Sejersen. He lived at the next place above us, so he took us to school for a few days until Malcolm could get a new rig and some more horses. One morning when Sejersen was taking us to school we got to school, jumped out of the sleigh and started for the school. He grabbed me and started to rub snow on my ears. I didn't like that at all. I was pretty mad at him for that because he was pretty rough and I couldn't get away from him. I found out later on that my ears had become frost bitten, and he did that to thaw them out.

A game of baseball with the Boy's King's Guards of the
Methodist Church. Frank is on the right.

Andrew Sejersen would keep a role in my life story. When I became a little older, often on Saturdays Sejersen would have me mix mortar for him because he was a bricklayer and mason and needed a helper. He showed me how he wanted it done. He was a man pretty particular how he wanted it and it had to be that way.

One Saturday, he was doing some plastering in a home down in Afton. We had the mortar box out in the backyard. I had to mix some mud and carry it through the kitchen and up the stairs to the room where he was plastering. He used 10-quart pails to carry it with.

The man who had hired Andrew came in. I thought this guy was an old man, but he wasn't very old at all. He saw me there and he asked, "What's that boy doing in there?"

Andrew said, "He's my helper". The guy said, "Don't want that boy around here. I'll do the mixing myself."

He started doing it, and Andrew said to me, "Just take a walk up town a bit." So I did. Andrew made a point to be on a sawhorse waiting for the mud. The guy was going as fast as he could go. Andrew would take that plaster and would stick up there; if I did it, it would be all over the floor. The guy did good work, but when Andrew heard the guy coming with more mud, he would sit down on the sawhorse, pretending to be waiting for more mud. In the meantime, another old guy came along, and they both couldn't keep up.

The old guy came back after lunch and asked Andrew, "Does that boy keep up with you?" Andrew answered, "He sure does!"

The old man wanted to see that so I got my job back, and, of course, Andrew was ready just about the time I got back with more mud. He timed it just so. The old fellow sat there shaking his head. Of course, he couldn't figure out how I could keep up. But that's the way Andrew was; he wanted things done his way.

After that, Andrew moved down to what is now Route 206; but that house sat way back from the road at the top of the cut. They moved in there and I continued to help Andrew quite a bit on Saturdays.

Lyon farm in 1919

It was 1928 or 1929, when we had a very cold winter and our fresh water spring froze up on the farm. We had to haul water from another spring in milk cans for the cattle and horses. Dad thought it was time to quit the dairy. So in 1929 he sold the dairy but kept the farm of course.

That's when I worked on the next farm up, a vegetable truck farm. The people that moved onto the place above us on Lyon Road, Dan Hunter and his wife, had work for me. One summer after my father sold the dairy, I worked up there for Dan. He had a truck farm and raised produce and took it to Johnson City to the market there. I always started with the work here on our farm before school and during the summer, and did his work in my other time.

A lot of things began to take place that I got into. Our school didn't have the sports programs that they do now. They only had football, baseball and basketball and that was all. This man came who was supposed to be a coach and a teacher, George Isle. He wanted to have something more going on. The school didn't have anything to do with it, but he organized a bunch of us boys into individual competitions. We started putting on exhibitions of wrestling and boxing.

They put cards in store windows around town when they were going to have a show. I boxed and wrestled, both. Bill Burton was a wrestler and they put our names on the cards. He was "Wild Bill Burton," a good name for him. I don't know where they got my name. I was "Box Car Doo," and I wrestled the "Mountain Man," Alvin Giles. There were quite a lot of us farmer boys. We were doing pretty well. I don't have any idea what they charged for people to come in to watch. The school allowed them to do it in the old auditorium. We had money enough to buy all the equipment we needed and everything else we had there, including the ring for the competitions.

But then some of the village fathers put a stop to it because somebody was going to get hurt. No one ever did, but probably their thought was correct. Anyway they stopped it. They had boxing and wrestling for a few more years after that as the school began to take on many more other sports.

I spent most of my growing up years working there on the family farm on Lyon Road. We raised some corn crops, some dairy, and potatoes mostly for our own use. We also raised cabbage. We used to plant seedbeds of cabbage plants for our own use. If it were more than we needed, people would come and get cabbage plants for their gardens. We raised corn for the farm animals and, of course, hay for the cattle and horses. We didn't have tractors, but we had four horses that we used for the farm work.

Brothers Paul, Richard on the horse, sister Ruth, and Frank
is in the wagon holding the horse reigns 1931

One Saturday in the wintertime I had picked up a lot of old scrap iron and things around on the farm. We had a little red sleigh that we used to haul milk in with one horse. I took that load of stuff to town to Frank Payne's. He lived next to where Bugbys live now, that last house down there. There was a barn down in back where he used to buy all kinds of scrap and furs and stuff like that. Of course, this was when the Old Road was there. To come into town we came down the main road that came out on Newton Avenue. The reservoir was up on that bank on the back of the road, and the overflow came down, and there was a slough under the road that came down to Newton Creek. Then in the wintertime that would freeze up; then the overflow would get in the road, go down the sleigh tracks, and down that hill.

On my way with the scrap, I went around the turn and started down the hill. It was all ice and the horse's feet got out from under him, and that sleigh with the iron in it pushed him right along down to the bottom of the hill. I thought I was going to get a ride, but when we got down where he could get up on his feet again, he got right up and went trotting along just as though nothing had happened. It scuffed the hair right off the backs of his legs. That was one of the capers I got into that could have turned out badly.

My cousin, Andy Doolittle, used to come up and we would visit back and forth quite a lot. We spent a lot of time together. One day he was up to our farm, and we were putting hay into the barn and as we backed out of the barn the horses scuffled along. They tripped on the stone over in the bridge there, and out came a swarm of bumble bees. They got after the horses and headed them right up the hill and had them run till they got tired of it (the bumble bees that is). Then the horses came back. We each had straw hats that we wore out beating off the bumblebees.

Frank as a young boy.

Probably two or three years later, I was up there alone on the farm and had most of the haying done. We had cut hay in the orchard. We had five or six acres of orchard, apple orchard. I had raked that out where I could get it with a hay loader, and I was getting that on the wagon when I saw this thick black cloud coming over from Coventry. I thought I'd better unhook and go to the barn. There was a twister that came up over there. We didn't see much of that, and that was the only one I had seen before. It came up over the hill and took every spear of hay off that wagon. I was on the front of the wagon driving the horses. There was hardly a breeze, but it went right through the orchard, and it destroyed the whole orchard. Then it went on down over the hill to the Pearl Street Extension. George Foster lived down there, and the house they lived in was severed a little bit from its foundation. The twister went across the river and was gone. That's all there was to it. That was another experience I will remember up there on the farm.

Then a little later there was a time when we got home from school, and I had to get the chores and the milking done. I always had to turn the cows out in the barnyard. We had a water trough out there where they could get a drink while we cleaned the barn. That night I opened the back door for the cows to go out. It had rained and frozen on the ground. There was quite a crust and the cows went out the door and they started getting in that ice. They panicked and went right on up over the hill, and I had quite a time rounding them up, and finally two of the neighbors' men came. I don't know how they found out about it, but anyway they came and helped me round them up again. It was dark and foggy but that was something. I never knew what kinds of things might happen on the farm.

In those days when they first started testing the cows for TB (tuberculosis). Everyone that had cows had some that they called "reactors." We had two or three. They're usually the best ones. My father started with ours, driving them over towards Loomis's, by Brackett Lake. We picked up two or three on the way. We got there and Ward had quite a few and some neighbors had dropped theirs in.

We started up what they now call the Ward Loomis Road, then went over on to the road that goes through Puckerville to Guilford. Carlton Loomis and I were driving. I think we had 35 or 36 cows by then. My father and Ward Loomis, who had a touring car, and his dog, were in the car. Carlton and I drove the cows over through and we came down Gospel Hill into Guilford, then right through Main Street in Guilford to the road that goes to Bainbridge now.

We went up to the railroad cattle yard. That's where we had to put the cows because they were going on the train to Chicago.

That was a long day. The dog didn't help us. He rode in the car all they way. At the end of the Ward Loomis Road is what they called a "summer road." It was open at that time. There were farms along this "summer road" and apple trees along side. This was where the cows wanted to go. We had quite a time getting them through there. Once we got them to Guilford, they went where we wanted them to go.

In those days, not much traffic was on the back roads. I don't think we saw a car all the way through. There was only the car that Ward and my father were riding in. After we got them in the stockyard, they took us into a little restaurant there to get something to eat. It had been at least five hours since we left our farm until we arrived in Guilford. I'd say it was at least eight miles we drove those cows.

Then, of course, when my father started to work away from the farm, and already had sold the dairy business, he rented some of the farmland to the Brandts that bought the farm where the Haddads lived. It had been many years; I don't know just how many years that our farm had been worked. When the Brandts got there, they plowed it up first thing. Then they got a nice new team of horses and had me doing the plowing and putting out the lime. So that took quite a while in the spring.

Jesse and Mabel with children Ruth, Richard, Paul and Frank
at the right, 1925 on the Doolittle farmhouse porch

Jesse second left and his logging team

Early Work Years

My father started his work for the Union Handle Company in Frankfort, NY. He was all over buying ash logs for the company. It was 1930 when they closed down. I don't know how he got together with Edsen C. Burdick at the Separator plant and Jacob Zell, who had been a foreman at the Frankfort plant, but the three of them got together. They formed the business Trico Handle and Lumber Company in Sidney. That was the first of June 1930. Each day after school, I went to work there at the mill for a couple of hours when they were just getting started.

Probably because my father knew him, I got acquainted with E. C. Burdick while I was still in school. I would go mow his lawn, with one of those push type mower with a little iron wheel. There was a grass terrace on each side of his lawn. Mr. Burdick had a long handled mower he used on those terraces, and another regular mower to use on the rest of his lawn. That was when I first got acquainted with him and his wife.

Frank's senior picture 1932 Bainbridge Central

Mrs. Burdick liked to play jokes on people. She didn't get out much because she couldn't hear. They had been buying Saratoga Vischi water by the case. After getting acquainted with us, we started bringing in spring water in gallon jugs from the farm. I'd bring in the water to set inside their entrance to the cellar. I'd put it to the side of the stairs that went up into their house. I would pick up the empty jugs as well. One day I was putting the water in there, she opened the door and said, "Oh, I thought it was somebody." I was about 16 years old at this time.

The Burdick's garage was like a 3-car garage. He had 2 cars and the other side was petitioned off for a little shop. There was a cellar under that part. There was a little manhole where you could go down a ladder. They kept vegetables there. He always bought these big cheeses, called it a wheel. He put it down there until it got the way he wanted it. When he cut one, he'd let us have part of it.

About 1935 a new first addition was built on the Bainbridge school, and things were pretty slack at the mill, and I had to find something else to do. So I went down there and got a job putting a new sewer line in for the new addition of the school building. The pay was 35 cents an hour digging the ditch by hand. It went from the building to Walnut Avenue and then down Walnut to Juliand Street.

Every morning I had a line of men there who wanted to work. Some of them didn't last until noon, but I stuck it out until it was done. The first day the guy that was doing the job, the headman, wanted me to be timekeeper. I had to go along to get the names of the men and keep track of their time and then get back digging. At night they had a big toolbox to put tools in. They had me see that the tools were all clean and dry and put in the toolbox before I went home. Then after we got started home, he had some kerosene flares to put on where we had been digging so people wouldn't fall in there. When he came to pay us, they gave me 40 cents an hour. That was the most money I'd ever seen. So I was there until we had the job done.

Then we went over on the other side of the school building. They had a little shack where men were lined up looking for work. So I went over there and got in line. I got a job there pouring concrete. They had a mixer and they were wheeling the cement up the planks and dumping it down in the forms and so I got onto that after I had watched them a little bit to see whether I could do that or not. They had two planks that they went over. Some were going along the plank and once in a while bounced their load and they'd go down in the hole. They hadn't back filled or anything, and that was the end of their job. I managed to do work there until the job was done.

There wasn't any more of that kind of work there so in the fall I got in with a group that was working out on farms, silo filling. I worked at that until that job was done.

Then the work was better at the mill, and I went back to the Trico Handle and Lumber Mill.

Bainbridge Village 1915

The Handle Works in Sidney, NY

Trico Handle and Lumber Company

I had started work at the handle factory in June 1930 while I was still in school. I was in the sawmill and handle factory until 1968. Before the mill was in Sidney, NY, the Glass factory was there and it burned and the bank had the property.

There were 3 men who formed the beginnings of the Trico Handle and Lumber Mill. My father Jesse Doolittle had come to know the lumber and timber business really well, and then 2 others who were interested in the new business. Mr. Burdick furnished the money to back the business and Jacob Zell would furnish the handle knowledge. Zell wasn't there very long. He was from Frankfort and had a family and wasn't there much. Burdick and I mostly ran the handle business by learning on the job.

The Handle Works in Sidney was next to the railroad. Actually it was between the O & W and D & H train tracks [Ontario & Western, Delaware & Hudson]. There were big doors on the side of the mill (see picture) where handles were loaded onto the boxcars of the train. The handles we made were tied into bundles. Sometimes just the dowels were loaded for ABW Handles and Tools in Parkersburg, West Virginia.

Edsen C. Burdick took me under his wing and I learned a lot about business from the way he conducted the business. I learned management, and how to make and use contacts for marketing.

There was a company down in Montrose that built machinery and he would take me with him sometimes. A Jewish man in the company there would buy out factories and rebuild the machines like new. That's where most of our machinery came from. He told me he wanted me to see the machinery because he said, "You are going have to run it."

I learned a lot of things like that to help me in the business. My father was familiar with the sawmill part and the timber end. Burdick and I handled the business this way right up to the night Mr. Burdick was killed.

Things were about to change at the mill.

It was New Year's Day, but we worked everyday; we didn't take holidays. The only holiday we had off was Christmas. There were no paid holidays in those days. That day was when the tragedy took place in Sidney.

When it happened I was still at the mill, we had worked the whole day. The train had stopped on the track in front, blocking my car so I couldn't get out after locking and closing up. The crossing was close to the mill. Mr. Burdick had just left, after returning to get his dinner pail he had forgotten. We visited a minute and he took off. In a few minutes one of the trainmen came down and wanted to know if I knew anyone who had just left.

Of course, it was Mr. Burdick. So he took me down to the engine that was halfway down to Main Street. Burdick's car was up off the ground and caught on the coupling of the front of the engine. Apparently the engine hit him broadside, knocked him out and he was down under the train. They figured his car must have got caught on the ties and he couldn't get across. I was supposed to identify him but there wasn't much to pick up. I recognized the car and knew who it was. He had been dragged under the train, and there was nothing left of him to identify. They scraped him off and put him in a bag. This was my father's and my partner in the mill.

They held me there until after 7 pm until the coroner was finished. Then they took me over to the funeral parlor. My father came while I was at the funeral parlor.

At that time Wilma and I were living at Twin Rivers Inn and I had no way to get word to them. We were newlyweds and I wanted to get home.

That was such a tragedy.

After they released my father and me, I went home. My father was to get up with the men who worked at the mill that we wouldn't be working the next day. There was one man who lived further down past Afton we couldn't get up with. I had to go down to tell him. That night I don't remember eating supper or anything else. It was all such a shock.

Then in 1940 I became a partner with my Dad, as Mr. Zell was also gone. Things like that, you live with for a long time.

Burdick had been doing the bookwork and had introduced me to ordering for the business. Now there was just my father, and he wanted me to go in with him so I made arrangements to do that. In 1940 I became a partner with my Dad.

We didn't have any money. Things had to change somehow. In January and February of 1941, we moved the sawmill from Sidney to Bainbridge. We moved everything. We didn't own the mill in Sidney because it belonged to the bank. One Sunday night we had a fire in there. The firemen did more damage than the fire did. The bank didn't want to fix anything, so that's when we decided we had to move to Bainbridge. The place in Sidney was a flat area down between an old bumpy railroad and the D & H. We always had to plan to be flooded at least twice a year. No one wanted to buy it. So we moved out to Bainbridge.

My father and I together ran the mill until we moved to a place here in town that was sold for taxes in 1941. We got it and planned to run only the sawmill part here and leave the handle business in Sidney. We didn't own the land up there, just rented it from the bank. But, as it turned out, we decided to move everything to Bainbridge. We built the building that's there now with a sawmill and a handle business. We knew the handle labor would become outdated; we started up the lumber year with building and roofing supplies in 1941. Once a month there was a lumber dealers meeting at night in Afton. I'd go to that and learned more about selling lumber.

I was now part owner and there came times, a lot of times, my father couldn't do the work. So he didn't have much to do with the company, only the sawmill on a temporary basis. I was basically running the mill. It was up to me to keep the business going.

My Uncle Perry Doolittle, my mother's brother came and helped out by running the sawmill. I hadn't run the sawmill much but I tail sawed for him, and ran the rip saw making the squares that went through the dowel machine for the handles. I ran all of that, handled the lathes and learned by doing it.

Perry lived in Otego, and he had quite a drive everyday. As the war was starting, Perry got a government job and he moved. The job was in Index, New York, and he worked there during the war. The government had a sawmill there to saw lumber for temporary quarters usually for officers. Tents were used by the enlisted troops.

Trico Handle and Lumber Company, in Bainbridge, NY

Jesse, my father ran the sawmill to make logs into planks that we made squares out of. It wasn't very long before he couldn't do very much anymore. He had a heart attack and couldn't do anything. At that time we had a lot of custom sawing to do. I had worked around in the sawmill and had learned a lot about it, so I took it over. We had a man doing the tail sawing, and I sawed about all the custom logs besides the handle logs.

So in 1950, I bought him out. My father had been in and out of the hospital, and it was costing a lot of money, and he didn't know how he was going to make out. I was the owner of Trico Handle and Lumber Company. So that's the way it went.

Our mill had made farm tool handles since the 1930s. We exported to the British Isles, Cape Town, South Africa, Argentina and New Zealand. We dealt a lot with British exporters. We also shipped handles for street workers in New York City, and shipped to West Virginia, handles for their farm tools.

There was a lot to keep up with in the mill. With the government taxing more and factory inspectors coming in to make sure things were done correctly I had to really keep on my toes.

We had put in a steam boiler so as to have steam heat at the mill. Changes had to be made after the inspector came in. These changes had to be done in order to keep the business going.

I got along with the men that worked there, no trouble with them. We had a good crew. Our lumberyard started to work well.

We bought hemlock and pine logs, sawed them and stacked them up to dry. Next, we'd get them into the lumber shed to sell. If we turned money over, we were lucky. If we did it twice a year, that's hardly enough.

I had been to some of the sawmills around and they would save their ash logs and bring them in here for us. That helped with getting more ash. Also, going around the county once in a while I'd see lumber stacked up to dry. I thought to buy this dry lumber, bring it in, run it through the planer and put it out in the shed to sell.

This could turn the money over faster. I started doing that. Sometimes, I'd bring that lumber in, run it through the planer, put it in the shed and sell some of it the same day. That made quite a difference. In a way it was cheaper to buy the lumber that way than it was to buy the logs, make the lumber and dry it. That helped quite a lot.

Briggs Lumber would buy the rough lumber from some of the smaller mills in the area and bring it to us and we'd run it through the planers for them. We did a lot of that for Briggs Lumber Company, that they took back and sold down there. We worked back and forth with them.

In those days the salesmen came to sell their products and the bar would be open. They encouraged you to have a drink with them. I had a lumber friend in Afton, who refused to do that, neither would I. Some of the business owners did take them up on the offer and woke up the next morning to see what they had bought, whether they needed it or not.

We had a saleswoman who came in about once a month to sell the lumber we had in the yard. They would tell me about new things. I would try some things. One new thing brought in was blacktop in bags. It came in a trailer load and I said we'd try a load of it. I thought it'd be left here quite a while. The guy who ran the "Shopper's Guide" let me put an ad in for this blacktop. The first I knew, the trailer load was gone. I decided to get another load, and that went.

By then, the hardware stores were selling it and so were other lumberyards. I didn't want to compete with them for that market. There was a little on hand and I didn't try very hard to sell that. I only sold what people wanted to come in to get. Things like this that I started, and then other businesses would pick it up.

The same happened with paint. This salesman came in and wanted me to sell paint. I didn't have room enough, really. But I did take in paint so if anyone wanted to order it, I could fill the order through the saleswoman. That way I didn't have to maintain an inventory.

This one other salesman said, "If you sell our paint, you'll be an exclusive dealer." That would be all right. Then the first I knew this man who lived up on Pearl Street who was a paperhanger and painter, had that paint. Bluler's Hardware also had this paint. The next time that salesman came around, I said, "No, I don't want to be the only dealer. Let the others have it."

Trico Handle and Lumber Company office in Bainbridge

Another product that turned out good was glass. There was a 30% mark-up on glass, and that sounded good. That was enough for me to learn how to cut glass. I learned how to handle it and it was a good deal. People would bring in their window sashes, and I would cut the glass and put it in, then putty it.

The nails came in hundred pound kegs. We had a lot of nail bins, in different sizes. I kept that filled up and sold a lot of nails to the contractors.

I gave them a little on them. Because of my inventory, I could get a good price on the nails. I could sell a keg to the hardware store for the same price they had to pay. The mill made a little profit here, and this added to my inventory.

When the war came along, we had to give up some of the exports to some of the countries. Argentina was one of the first because Nazi Germany had taken over. Another one was New Zealand, which was British.

We had become acquainted with some of these middlemen they called "Jobbers". A lot of these merchandise companies we had to go through a "Jobber" to sell their products. So I went through these jobbers, and they got the orders.

During the war we ordered through one of them in Philadelphia that sold a lot of handles for boat hooks. The Jobber had the government contracts. They'd send the socket to our lumber mill so we could make a handle to fit. The handles were 8 feet long and with the hook at the end of the handle, they could push or pull the boat when leaving or landing. They were needed during the war and were used on the PT boats. We shipped them to Baltimore, which is where the ships were. We became very much educated in marketing. It all worked out pretty good until after the war.

The guys started coming home and wanted to build a house, and couldn't borrow money. That's when the government came up with the Veteran Loans. The government told the veterans where they had to buy their materials. Companies couldn't use native lumber anymore. It had to be western lumber. That cut into the building suppliers.

I began selling wood burning stoves. I sold a lot of them. We had bought one to use at the office of the mill to burn up some of the slab wood. The wood stove company wrote me that I was the dealer for the stoves. I didn't want to be the dealer, but they insisted. Finally, I told them if they would send me the orders, I'd take care of them. That's the way I did it until finally someone else wanted to be a dealer. If they wanted to buy the stove parts I had at the mill, then they could take it over, and I'd be rid of that.

With some of the machinery we had there at the mill, I made some of the moldings. Some were saved from the sawed pine; the edgings could make the moldings that were sold in the lumberyard. I had a big box of knives that came with the machine that Jim Thorpe had.

He didn't want it anymore so I set it up to make moldings. A lot of these old houses had moldings made just for that house such as in the Victorian style houses. The carpenters at that time made the moldings by hand. If they wanted to restore an older house, those moldings couldn't be bought anywhere. I managed to fish out some of those knives, get them set up so I could make some of those special moldings. A lot of those moldings and materials had not cost us. Otherwise, the pieces would have gone into the woodpile. These were the kind of things that kept the mill going.

We had a customer, Mark Cooper, who had the hardware in Bainbridge; noticed there were kits made for little girls. He decided he'd like some small rolling pins for children and put in baskets around in the stores to sell locally. We made thousands of them and put around the state. We also made some special rolling pins for Italians who lived in Sidney. They came in to ask for some longer ones that they could used to roll out their pasta. We used a speed lathe to make 4 or 5 in a minute. They were well liked. The rolling pins were made from maple or cherry wood. We used mostly ash lumber to make wagon tongues. Picket fences were another product made from mostly ash trimmings.

I watched pretty close the people who wanted to get materials and pay later. We didn't have any credit balances on the books in 1968, when I thought the mill had been sold. It had all been collected.

My father would let some people have materials and pay later. Then he would go to them to get paid.

One man across the river bought an old house and did a lot of work on it. My father let him have all he needed, and then we didn't see him anymore. I was hauling logs above there one day and saw a pile of logs in his yard. I looked at them and thought to myself, "We can make some lumber out of those."

I told my father that I'd go get those logs, bring them in here, make some lumber from them and get his bill caught up. He didn't like it. He said, "He'll have the police on you."

I said, "No, he won't. I don't think he wants to deal with the police any."

I went up and got 2 loads of logs, brought them in, kept them separate in case he wanted to come in and discuss things. He never came down.

After quite a long time, we sawed the logs, got the lumber and kept track of the money. It came to a little more than what his bill was. The mill came out ahead that time.

We had another time with some people from Guilford who were noted for not paying their bills. They had to build a new milk house. They came to get some materials and we let them have what they needed. They didn't come in to pay. After quite a while, they started bringing in logs. They'd bring in a load of logs, and I'd measure them and told them this will go right onto your bill. They didn't like that and I said that's the way it has to be. I told them we have to pay for those materials that you got. If we don't get paid, how are we going to pay? This is the only way we can do this. It'll help you. That went along well until they were caught up. I knew where they were getting the logs from a man I knew in Guilford. One load they brought in looked different from the others.

I saw this fellow one-day and asked him, "How are you getting along with your log cutters?" He says, "Oh, good. They have to bring a load down my driveway when they come out with a load."

I asked, "Do you know how many loads they take out?"

He answered, "Oh, yeah, I keep track of it."

I thought that a little odd, because some of the logs I was getting had come out the back way. This was going to get a little fishy.

I kept those logs separate and it wasn't very long before the police came. They wanted to know if these people had brought logs in. I said, "Yes," and showed them the logs and where I had measured them.

Well, it turned out that one load out of four had gone down his driveway and the rest went out the other way.

After the police had taken an inventory, then we could go ahead and use the logs. That was after they were all paid up. My father didn't like those kinds of deals, but what are you going to do? Money had to be in the office every Saturday for payroll.

The handle factory probably employed 20 at the most. Harry Mulwane worked for me about 20 years. My mother Mabel worked in the mill office until my father couldn't work any longer. Then she stayed home to take care of him.

Frank on homemade Doodle Bug at the saw mill

Then in 1968 a man came along and wanted to buy the mill. We knew the handle business did not have a good future and the making of the handles would become obsolete. We were making tool handles at that time. We had turned the mill into the retail lumberyard too, and I was doing pretty well. We had expanded into roofing materials and other hardware. But he came and wanted to buy it, and there wasn't anyone else who would be interested in it. So it got down to the final papers, and he wanted to lease it for a year to see how it would go, and that's what happened. He had me get somebody to run it for him, and that's when we got Chauncey Stone there. He ran it for a year.

Wilma Gustavson 1936 school picture

Someone Most Important to Me

I was in high school in 1930 when this girl and her parents came up from New York City. They came to Bainbridge Central High School. I was up stairs on the second floor of the school, and through the window I saw them. There were some other fellows with me. To us it looked like they had just landed, because they came up from Brooklyn. That's the first time I saw that girl. I had no idea that I'd ever get near her. Anyhow she was 13 years old at the time. Later on, that's the girl I married, Wilma Gustavson.

At that time they lived at Welcome Inn (Twin Rivers Inn of Bainbridge then) because her parents, Verner and Jenny Gustavson, had bought the inn. She had to attend the Bainbridge School.

Then they first started going to church, and they had tried different ones in town. They ended up there in our First Presbyterian Church. Of course, I saw her from a distance various times at school and at church.

One night about 2 years after Wilma came to Bainbridge, I was going to Sidney to work a few hours in the handle factory after school. I came by and saw her walking along the road, a scrawny little kid then. I stopped to see if she wanted a ride. She said, "No," she didn't want a ride, so I went away.

When she got home and talked with her mother, she was mad that she had to walk all the way home. When she told her mother I had stopped, she asked, "Do you know him from school?" She said, "Yes, and we go to the same church." Her mother told her she knew me well enough to ride home with me.

The church the Gustavsons went to before in Brooklyn was a Swedish church and was more like a congregational church. In those days, the sections of the city of Brooklyn had their own church. Such as the Swedish, the Italian, the Irish each also had their own shops. But when they moved to Bainbridge, they didn't have the same kind of neighborhoods. They went to the Congregational Church, the Methodist and the Baptist church.

They came to the Presbyterian Church in Bainbridge when a couple of us boys were ushers. We had to know where certain people wanted to sit and wouldn't want to put someone else in there. We were ushers all the time. When the Gustavsons came they said our church people were the most friendly and made it their church, and joined.

We had people in those days at church if someone was in their seat, they'd have to move. They usually got there at the last minute. One of them was the Ives family. They sat right up front and there had to be room there so if their son came, he could sit with them. We didn't want to put anyone else there except this family. They were always there.

There were others the same way, wanted to sit in the same seats every Sunday. Harold Lord and his mother were Quakers and they went to church there. We always kept their seat empty for them to come in. They were always there.

Towards the end of my ushering there was another couple I remember well. Walt Royder was one of the VIPs at the Borden Company. At that time his wife was playing the organ and needed a seat nearby so she could join him after playing. Before that, the preacher's wife had always needed a seat. The Peckhams, Charlie and his wife liked to have a seat saved, too.

Another part of my ushering job was to run the air bellows for the organ. I was in the little cubbyhole in back of the organ. Sometime after that, the church put in an electric pump for the organ. The bellows was like a big bag that stayed full of air. But when she started playing the organ, I'd have to start pumping to keep air in the bag. I couldn't see what was going on except to keep air in that bag. Basically, I had to stay back there the whole service to make sure the air bag was full. It was almost steady pumping, and I couldn't doze off!

We boys were doing our job ushering and the Gustavsons thought that was pretty nice. Wilma and her parents joined the church at the same time. It was good that we were both members of the same church before we married.

By this time being a high school graduate, 2 younger boys had taken over the ushering duties. Wilma and I were involved in Sunday school and other activities together.

She was probably about 15 years old when I stopped by the Twin Rivers Inn one evening to get some gas on my way home from the mill. They had gas pumps there and her mother came out and pumped the gas. I asked her if it'd be all right if I stopped by later to ask Wilma to go to the movies. Well, first, I didn't know that movies were a "no-no". She froze right up and I went right on home.

First I had supper and then went back to see if Wilma could go to the movies. Apparently, she hadn't been anywhere, only to church and to school. So when I arrived they talked it among themselves, to include her sister Olga. Finally they let her go. I took her to the movies, brought her back and I went home.

My first car was a 1929 Dodge, which I had when Wilma and I were first dating. One evening I had driven over to Wilma's, and we were sitting in Wilma's mother's house on a couch. Her mother had an alarm clock in the kitchen and would walk through the living room winding her clock. This being at night was her way of letting me know it was time to go home. So I went home.

My first car was a 1929 Dodge Victory

I didn't know then that I was going to marry her and live with her for 68 ½ years. That's the longest career I've had!

When Wilma finished high school she went to Albany Business College. For some reason or another, I have no idea why, I made a few trips up to Albany. One of the trips I had just bought a new car and it had a governor on it. In those days they put a governor on the new cars to break them in. It could only go 25 mph. I think it was about 500 miles to Albany. Dick, my younger brother, went with me.

Frank and Wilma school days 1932

We worked until noon at the mill that Saturday and I had to go home to get ready. Dick and I started out and we got up to Colesville at the top of the hill. There were some cabins and we stayed in one of them that night. There were no motels in those days. Then Sunday morning we got out early and went on to Albany.

We arrived to the apartment where Wilma lived with two other girls. But they weren't up so we went over to Louise's house. Louise was a cousin and had been here to visit a lot and she had a niece who knew a guy who had a riverboat. She took Dick and me down to the riverboat, for a tour of the boat, and we came back. The girls were not up yet. We decided to go over to Schenectady, where a cousin of my mother lived and we knew her quite well. We went over to say "Hello" to them and came back. It was getting close to Sunday noon and we stopped again at Louise's and they were getting ready to go on a picnic up to Indian Ladder. They said we could go with them.

I said, "Guess we'd go back down to see if the girls were up." They were up this time, and Wilma got ready and went with me. We went up with Aunt Ida to the picnic. Aunt Ida was a sister to Wilma's mother and she lived in Brooklyn. We would have to go there sometimes to visit.

When we left, it was near time for Dick and me to start home. We took Wilma back to her place. Why I ever went back to Albany again I don't know, but I did.

The next time I had my car all broke in by then. I took Wilma's father and mother up to visit. They wanted to go so all of us went into Albany. Wilma had moved. Louise had found her an apartment on the same street where she lived. It was down the road a ways. We went over there and this woman had a room full of folks but no place for me. She fixed it so I slept on the kitchen floor with the mops. The next morning, Sunday, they wanted to go to Wilma's mother's cousin who lived in Shushan, New York.

We got out of there and went to Shushan. We were there for dinner, and then had to leave because we had to get Wilma back to Albany and we had to get back home.

I don't know how many weeks went by between times but Louise's husband worked for Montgomery Ward in a little place north of Albany. He got Wilma a job up there. She was working up there besides finishing up her school. When she completed school, she came home and went to work in Scintilla. This was after the middle of 1937.

During the next year Wilma and I dated. Usually we went to the movies together at Smally's Theater in Sidney and then back home, to her house. We would also go on little rides around the countryside and stop somewhere to visit or stop somewhere for a meal. Also we'd go on picnics. When I look back on that time, I think this whole thing must have been planned ahead by someone. I have no idea why it happened the way it did. I think Wilma's father had a little something to do with it.

Wilma told me later on that her mother told her, "Now you've made your bed, you've got to lie in it." Her mother wasn't too excited about me but I kind of grew on her. Some bad feelings had gone back to their life in

Brooklyn. Wilma's father would buy a place, fix it up and sell it. At that time Verner Gustavson would sponsor some of the people coming from Sweden. In those days they had to make sure they had a place to live and that they could get a job by a certain time.

Quite a few of these young men coming over had known the family in Sweden. So they would come here. That's how the one came that married Olga, Wilma's sister. She was 18 years old and had a baby. So they got married. I always figured the problem between them and baby daughter Ramona was they blamed the baby for having to get married. To me that's the way it looked. Ramona stayed in our lives until she was about 8 years old.

One time when I was going with Wilma some, she had a girlfriend coming up from Brooklyn in the summer. She was coming into Oneonta on the bus. I took Wilma and Ramona in to Oneonta to pick up her girlfriend. We got up there and picked her up. She was to stay with Wilma's folks a couple of weeks. Wilma's aunt and her youngest daughter Dagny were nurses. They thought Wilma ought to be a nurse. This was in the summertime. She decided she would go to Buffalo for an interview to be a nurse. So I took Wilma and her girlfriend to Buffalo, New York. While she was in the interview, her girl friend and I toured Buffalo.

For the night, we got rooms in a house and mine was downstairs and theirs was upstairs. My room was all right but they had trouble with bedbugs in their room. We only had to stay over one night. We came back home, and it wasn't long before her girlfriend had to go back home. The Gustavsons took her back to Oneonta for the bus.

I continued to call on Wilma a few times. I guess I must have popped the question. That's what she wanted. I think she had planned that a long time before. I hadn't thought too much about getting married. Anyway, it happened. Later on we got a little closer together.

At the end of May, on Memorial Day, we were to get married. We used to call it "Decoration Day."

On May 28, 1938, I married Wilma Gustavson. Our marriage wasn't a big affair. The Reverend Orvis married us in her parent's house, which was across the road from the Inn. My mother and father were there at the ceremony. Ove Munk, who had been my buddy since starting school, was my best man. Wilma had her sister Olga as matron of honor. A lady from Sidney played the piano. Wilma's family were there: her mother and father, sister Olga and her husband, two cousins Agnes and Agni from Brooklyn and their mother who was Wilma's aunt, and sister to Wilma's mother. There was an Uncle Anton and his wife Esther and their little girl Violet about 10 years old there as well. This uncle was a brother of Wilma's mother.

Verner and Jennie with daughter Olga Gustavson 1917

After the marriage ceremony, our reception was held at the Twin Rivers Inn. We left the reception and walked towards the car. That's when we saw what had been going on outside with the car. We had a 1937 Plymouth coupe, which had a rumble seat commonly called a "mother-in-law" seat. Some smart alecks had tied roller skates and I don't know what all. Anyway there were wires underneath and in the exhaust pipe a potato had been plugged into it. We got away and were inside the car. One window wasn't closed so we got a lot of rice in the car.

When I started the car, it blew the potato out and we went away towards Bainbridge. At that time there was a wide place in the road where the state had their oil drums that they used on the roads. I swung around in there and right back up the road towards Sidney. There was a gas station as you come into Sidney. I knew the guy that owned it. The door was open where their pit was for changing oil. I pulled in there and he shut the door. They came roaring up through town and never found us again. He got the stuff unfastened from the car and we started for Atlantic City. Wilma really wanted to go to Atlantic City, New Jersey for our honeymoon.

When we first came into Atlantic City it was getting dark and were thinking of a place to stop. We came to this house that had a light on and it was a Justice of the Peace. We stopped there and they put us up for the night.

The next morning, we drove on down into Atlantic City and came to a road that went out to an island. We decided to go out to see the island and found 3 little landings where fishing boats came in. We hadn't been out there very long before there wasn't any road. The tide had come up. We stayed there that night. They had a little restaurant so we could eat some dinner.

The next day we went up to the boardwalk. She wanted to do that. So we went that far and soon had to head for home because we both had to be to work the next day. We didn't see a lot but were able to have our honeymoon at the boardwalk in Atlantic City.

We arrived home late in the evening. That was quite a ways to travel in those days. I usually worked ½ day on Saturdays, but had taken that day off to get married. Therefore my paycheck was short. Wilma worked that next week and then Scintilla laid off all the married women. Right away she got a job at Kent's Store. She worked there a little while until Scintilla called her back. That worked out pretty good.

In those days if you worked full-time, it was a 40-hour week. I was working a 50-hour week at the mill and Wilma was working 40 hours at Scintilla. My pay was $16.80 for the week and hers was $!4.40. So we didn't have a lot of money to start our married life.

That first year after we were married, we lived there in Twin Rivers Inn. The Gustavsons had put in a bar to make things neat and so Wilma told her mother that the first year after we were married we would stay there and help them. They were trying to sell the inn and we would stay there until it was sold.

Wilma and her niece Ramona in front of our house, on Route 7 to Sidney, NY. Twin Rivers Inn (right) is across the road from the house (left).

We lived in Wilma's room that opened up in the front of the house, which was directly across the road from the inn. Her parents lived here too. The location was very convenient so we could be there to help out.

The Gustavsons needed a bar tender and apparently bar tenders drank quite a lot. Most of the time Wilma was working at Scintilla and I was working at the mill in Sidney. At night when we were there, we always helped, she waited tables and they had me tending the bar. I had done nothing like that before.

I had a little pad of notes that I could look at when asked to mix drinks. I studied that quite a lot, and got away with it. If anybody came in and wanted a drink I didn't know about, I'd say, "How would you have me mix that?" Then they'd tell me. So I got away with it.

Saturday night was a big night. They had a fiddler come in and had dancing, round and square dancing. I would tend the bar from probably 7:00 until after midnight.

I was also bouncer. Having been a boxer and wrestler in high school, I had learned a few things about thwarting some bad and angry behavior. So I thought I could handle anything that came along and I did.

There were a couple of incidences that could have escalated in to something terrible, but I caught it before it went too far and took care of it.

This one Saturday I arrived there early that night. There were 4 guys at the bar that had been "coon" hunting. They were a little bit loaded but they were all right. They were talking about "coon" hunting adventures.

Well, two big black guys came in and they overheard the hunters say something about "coons". Right away I could see they were ready for trouble. So I caught them before they got in very far. I told them these guys were talking about their days hunting, of "raccoons". The 4 hunters never realized that the black guys were in there. The black guys decided they'd leave and that took care of that issue. Whew-ew-eee!

Then one Saturday night Jiggs Alford came in. He was like two people. He was different when he'd been drinking. He'd had all he needed before he came into the inn. I was kind of watching him because he and two of his buddies had torn up the hotel in town. The people in Bainbridge couldn't stop him anymore.

Jiggs was alone when he came in. I had known him quite a while as a farmer in our area. He came to the bar, and I said, "I can't serve you anymore. You've had all you need. You go over there and sit down for a while. There's a table and chair." So he did. But he didn't stay and came around to the bar again and ordered his drink. I said, "I can't give you one." Well, he decided to get it himself. He started around the end of the bar.

I said, "Don't come around here." We had a steel bar that was used to break the bottoms out of liquor bottles so they couldn't be used again, and I picked it up.

I'm telling you, "Don't come around here." He kept right on coming. I didn't want to hurt him, so I laid down the steel bar and when he got around where I could get hold of his arm, I twisted it right around behind him. He turned right around and someone opened the side door and out we went!

There were two steps down and he missed them. Then down he went into the parking lot that was cinder. He went right down there on his hands and knees. I waited, didn't know if he was hurt. He got up and I didn't know what he was going to do. Instead of coming towards me, he went right through a barberry hedgerow, full of thorns, to a driveway that went down to the cellar. I went down there because I thought he'd be hurt. When he finally got up, I asked him if he was all right. He said, "Yeah, I'm all right!"

He had this little pick-up truck that he climbed into. I thought about taking the keys out, but I watched him a few minutes and he went right to sleep. I could see he was all right, and I went back inside.

Some of the guys in there said he'd be back and kill me next time. I said, "He'll have to come in here to do it." But he never did.

That's the second incident that could have escalated into some terrible. In those days, I was pretty rugged. I thought I could handle most anything and I did.

That was the only time I ever had any real trouble at all. The rest of the time people were pretty reasonable, and just having a good time.

Late that night at 1:00 AM, we always had to clean up and then go to the house. On my over to the house, I saw Jiggs was still in his truck. I left his keys with him and in the morning, he was gone. It was many years before seeing him again.

While living here in Bainbridge, I was on the jury downtown for a trial. Jiggs and his buddies were not supposed to be in town. Bill Payne had picked up one of them. Jiggs was in his car downtown and he wanted to have a trial for his buddy. Clyde Hitchcock was the judge and I was one of the jurors. He said he had come to see that his buddy got justice. Bill said, "You can sit in the back but we don't want any disturbance back there. And when it's over, you leave." So that worked all right.

When the trial was all finished, the buddy decided he wasn't going to pay his fine. Bud Marshall, who was Justice of the Peace, said, "You'll have to spend the night in our jail. Either pay up or go to jail." Jigg's buddy said, "I have to get home to tend to my chores."

It was maybe 7:30 or 8:00 at night, and Clyde said, "You should have thought about that earlier." When he saw there was no other way out, he threw down the money and paid. Jiggs and his buddies left. When I went to go out of the town hall, they were sitting there on the steps that went upstairs. Jiggs got up and wanted to shake my hand. He said, "I'm glad you came to see that my buddy got justice." I was glad to see that this all ended peacefully and we were on good terms.

We lived there at the Twin Rivers Inn a little more than a year when the Gustavsons sold the inn. They moved to a big farm near Oxford, NY. Neither Wilma nor I had many belongings so it was easy when we had to move.

A couple that had been coming Saturday nights to the inn had a place a little below town. They wanted to go down to Volonia Springs to run a gas station. They wanted us to move into their house, which was a little cottage. So we did. This cottage was across from where the electric plant is today in Bainbridge.

Wilma's sister, Olga Ideman, had a daughter named Ramona who was about 6 years old at this time. She was living with Wilma's folks in the inn. She knew me more than she knew her own father. She was with Wilma and me a lot during the past year.

Wilma was maybe 11 or 12 years old when her sister's baby came along. Wilma's mother and Wilma were taking care of the baby, and not Olga. I thought maybe that was the reason Wilma didn't want any children of her own. We always had small and grown up children around and enjoyed having them. Whether it was nieces or nephews or neighbor children, we had a lot of fun with the children.

We took Ramona with us because she wanted to stay with us and so did her parents. That worked out pretty good; she could go to school when Bainbridge schools were first centralized. The bus would pick her up there in the morning and at night they arranged it so that the bus went up the river road to Sidney and let her off in Sidney where I could pick her up. Wilma was working second shift. Sometimes we'd have to get groceries, then go home and get us supper.

One night, Max Spawn who I've known since school days, came down. I was going to have hamburgers. The way I made them was to pat the meat out in my hands into a patty and put them in the frying pan to cook. Ramona kept watching me and when Wilma came home that night, she had to tell her about my getting their supper. Ramona said, "He doesn't know how to make hamburgers."

Wilma's mother had this little form that she used to press the hamburger meat into when she made them at the inn for customers. I didn't have the form, and just patted them out and fried them that way. They tasted just as good.

We were there about 4 to 5 months when the couple who were letting us rent their cottage wanted to come back. So we drove over to Sidney and rented an apartment there. Then they changed their mind again and wanted us to stay. We weren't going to stay there because we had the apartment in Sidney and we both worked in Sidney. That was the decision we made.

At that time Ramona was about 8 years old when her parents, Olga and Leonard Ideman bought a place in Masonville and decided she was big enough now to take care of herself. So she had to go live with them. She didn't want to leave and we didn't want her to go, either. There was nothing we could do. Ramona lived with her folks from then on.

Ramona had to change schools and it was difficult for her to live there with her parents. As soon as she turned 16, she left home. She met someone by the name of Richards and apparently he was a lot like her father. It was like she stepped out of the frying pan into the fire. Conditions were not good, and she became a different person. They had a little girl named Christine and after a while they started coming to our house to visit, and sometimes to eat a meal. Ramona's husband was working in Scintilla at the time. The department where he worked moved to South Montrose, so they had to go down there to live.

I took my truck and moved them to an apartment in a big farmhouse. They weren't there very long when they took off and no one knew where they went. We didn't hear anymore from them in quite a long time.

Finally, Wilma's sister heard from them and they were in Arizona. They were in pretty bad shape, I guessed. Olga's daughter Ann and her father went out to see them and helped out some. From there they moved to California. We never heard anymore from Ramona at all. But the Gustavsons went out to visit when they heard Ramona was very sick in bed and died.

In total time, Ramona had been living with us for about 2 years at the inn, in the cottage and our apartment in Sidney, which includes some time before Wilma and I were married. She had those memories with us when she was little. Later on Ramona's daughter Christina married and had 2 little boys, and she came to see us when we lived in Florida, several times. The daughter told us that she had to raise her 2 brothers because Ramona had died of poor health.

One of these grandsons came to Florida to see us even though we had never met them. Ramona apparently still had her happy memories when she was with us and relayed these times to her daughter and grandsons. It was good that she wanted to visit and have her sons meet us.

Our apartment in Sidney was a duplex and lived on one side. We had a kitchen, dining room and living room downstairs. Upstairs there were two bedrooms and a bathroom. Then we had a back porch and a front porch. It must have been November the first time it got cold; the apartment had a pipe less furnace with just one register. I went down into the cellar to start a wood fire in the furnace. It burned coal, too. The smoke came up through the register and filled the apartment. Something was wrong there, so I took a look at it. Come to find out there was a chunk broken out of the chamber of the furnace. That had to be fixed because we had to have heat.

I got some furnace cement, put the piece back in, and cemented in place. That seemed to be all right and it worked well. The guy that owned the duplex lived down in Binghamton and people had told me that they couldn't get anything done around there. There were a lot of things in the house that needed to be fixed. The neighbors could not get him to do anything around there.

We paid $20.00 a month and when I sent the money in for the rent, I wrote a note with it telling him about the issue with the furnace and deducted it. He didn't drive but had his daughter bring him up to Sydney just to see me. I showed him the out side; the back porch had pieces broken out with a pail sitting over it. The chimney went up the backside of the house and leaked some around where the chimney went up through the edges of the roof. I showed him those things and he said, "I didn't know anything about it."

Apparently they had never told him. He says, "Well, we have to get this fixed." He got somebody right on it, fixed everything right up. He was glad I had fixed the furnace and the other things I needed to fix. He was all right.

For hot water we had a little stove down in the cellar, which burned coal. We got along all right. The owner was surprised that so much had to be done. I don't know why the neighbors said they couldn't get him to do anything. His daughter had brought him up there, and when he saw what needed to be done, he went ahead and got someone to do it.

The people who lived in the other side of the duplex had lived there quite a while. A man and his old maid sister and his grown-up son lived there. His sister worked for a lawyer there in Sidney and he worked in

Scintilla as well as his son. On their side was a 2-car garage. Part of that was ours, but we never used it.

That was New Street and it went clear through to the next street. At that time there was a feud going on. Some did not want that street there, and a fence would go up sometimes. Then the fence would come down. Finally, the village closed it entirely. We were at the end of the street. On the other side was a single-family house. It was a nice house with nice neighbors.

So we rented the duplex in Sidney until Hudson Lyon offered to sell us a place to build a house next to his on Kirby Street.

Pines Farm which was an early name for the Doolittle farm on Lyon Road, 1938. L to R are Will Davis, Hudson and Jannette Lyon, Frank and Wilma Doolittle, Mabel and Jesse Doolittle and Albert Sheldon standing behind Frank.

Frank at home, 5 Kirby Street, Bainbridge, NY, in 2014

5 Kirby Street

After we went to Sidney to live, we didn't have any idea about building a house. We didn't have any money; all we could do was pay our rent.

Hudson Lyon wanted us to buy his place next to his house on Kirby Street and build this house. The way it turned out he would back us, which made it possible. Wilma and I talked it over quite a bit. We didn't have to pay him much on the lot, only $20.00 a month as long as we lived there.

Our first place, the Twin Rivers Inn had running water, electric light and the same with the house where we lived across the road. It was a great adventure starting out and building a new house for both Wilma and me.

When I was in high school, we had one subject called "Commercial Arithmetic." In this class I learned how to paper and paint, to plaster and figure out rolls of paper needed. These came in handy later on in the mill business. I don't think they have anything like that anymore in the high schools. Today if someone is needed to paint, paper or plaster, they hire someone to do it. This commercial arithmetic also was put into use with our new house in figuring how much of each material was needed.

This was in 1940 and we were just starting to think about the lumberyard. We were getting acquainted with these salesmen that came around and I could get materials that way. It would be delivered right here to the site for our house. The door, windows and hardwood flooring we had to get. The subfloor was tongue and grooved hemlock. All the sheeting we did down at the mill.

We didn't have the money to build the house. We went to the bank and Mr. Kirby was there, head of the bank. I talked with him about it and what we had in mind, and what we wanted to do. He said, "Well, my boy. You don't have any collateral." I couldn't get any money.

At that time, Norwich Bank was taking it over and I said, "Maybe Mr. Brooks would come over from Norwich." He had an office upstairs over the bank. He said, "I'll tell you when he comes."

Apparently he had come a few times to the bank and I didn't hear anything. The Trico Handle Company had their business there in the bank. One morning my father came down to the bank and came to Sidney. He told me, "Mr. Brooks is down there."

I took right off and went down. Shirley Stewart was one of the tellers and she said, "Can I help you?'

I said, "I don't know, but thought I'd like to see Mr. Brooks." She opened the gate and I went upstairs to see Mr. Brooks.

He was busy so I waited a little while. When he came, I told him what I had and what I wanted to do. We talked about it quite a little bit. Finally, he went to his desk. You wait there just a few minutes. When he came back, he had a checkbook. He said, "You can start drawing on that any time you want to."

I wasn't quite ready for that. That's the way it started in 1940. We started building the house in October 1940.

I had no idea how much money I could draw on. Mr. Brooks had told me to start drawing on it. He had given me a checkbook. I talked with Mr. Brooks several times and he reminded me, "You draw what money you have to."

First they had to dig the hole for the foundation. Andy Sejersen did all the cement work. He did the cellar floor and walls and the fireplace. Wilma had to have a fireplace. The large stone in the middle of the fireplace was in the field across from Andy's house. He brought it down and placed it there. The rest of the stone came from the Bluestone quarry in Unadilla. To start with he asked me, "Do you want to get the rest of the stone for the fireplace?"

I said, "No, you know what you need for the stonework." So I got the heater part from Norwich, which has intake vents for cool air at the bottom, then releases the warm air out of top vents.

So he went up one day with his pick-up truck and picked out some stones from the refuse, what he wanted and came down and dumped it on the living room floor. They had the house all closed in and were still working inside. The subfloor of the first floor was done. I asked, "What is that pile on the floor?" He said, "That's your fireplace." That's the way it turned out.

I knew Andy quite well because I had worked for him when I was maybe 14 years old. They lived in the next house up. He had me to work on Saturdays mixing mortar for him. He showed me how he wanted it mixed and that's the way it had better be! I knew how he was and if he picked out what he wanted it would be best.

It was the same time Oris Coe was building a house down Julian Street and he saw what I had done here. He then went up and got a whole truckload full of stones for his fireplace. Andy was going to build his too. Andy went down and looked at it and said, "No, I can't use it." He had to get all good cut stone. I knew it was better for him to pick it out, because after working with him, that was the only way to have it. It worked out all right for me but not for Coe. He had more than just a chimney, but part of where the chimney was laid up was stone too.

Wilma's father, Verner Gustavson, and another man built the house. They had just finished building the post office in Oxford and had no other work planned. They came and built this house.

"Why don't you get the rough lumber delivered right here and run it through my planer?" Jim Thorp said. So that's what I did. I came down nights after supper with my dual-wheeled trailer, run lumber up there through the planer and get it back to the job site the next day. This was done for all the lumber in the house.

Jim Thorp knew what I was planning to do, and wanted to help. He had gone into woodworking. He had a 3-sided planer that could tongue and groove, and another little planer that could plane one-side. That's when he said I could buy the rough lumber and run it through his planers. He got in touch with someone that could deliver the rough lumber for $27.00 per 1,000.

At that time we lived in Sidney. So after supper, I had a 2-wheeled trailer I pulled behind my car. I went down to Jim's and run lumber 1st through the one-side and then through the 3-sided, all the frame, 2 x 4's, 2 x 6's, 2 x 8's all through the 3-sided planer.

Clyde Hitchcock across the river had a dairy and peddled milk here in town. He had made arrangement with Jim to keep his hands cleaned up. All the shavings I had made, Clyde took for bedding. That worked out pretty good.

I had all the lumber planed and brought up to keep the work going the next day on our house. That worked out well. We had started to make arrangements to get material from the lumberyard for flooring, doors and windows.

Wilma's father would tell me what they needed. So the next day I'd get that all up here that night to keep him going in the daytime. I handled every piece in this house more than once, except the fireplace.

We talked with salesmen from Babcock Hinds and Underwood, a hardware company in Binghamton who sold retail and wholesale, to buy 100 lb. keg of nails.

The Wood Glass Company in Syracuse, NY, delivered right to the work site. We charged it up to the Trico Handle and Lumber Company. Of course, we had to pay for it. It was different from buying from a regular lumber company. I got a break on everything. The wallboard and everything was there at the company.

Wilma's father laid out the house. We had one of those precut home catalogs. He took it and fixed the house he thought would fit in between the two houses on each side. That's how it turned out the way it is now. Thorp and Hayes made the front door, the storm door and the screen door. He was a woodworker and made them there on the lot. Thorp and Hayes had made all the windows for the Trico Lumber Mill. They had to remake the front door because the winter weather with the cold and moisture warped the door. So they took off the door and put in steel rods and it stayed straight after that.

Whenever color or decorator items had to be picked out, Wilma did that. She chose the curtains and had interest in the hardwood floors in the living room, dining room and hallway and also in the hallway upstairs. The upstairs was all open with the rafters and two by fours.

When we moved in, I finished the upstairs when there was time. I spent a lot of days up there after supper. I got it the way it is now with two bedrooms, a half-bath and a pretty good-sized hallway. There's a lot of storage space under the rafters on both sides.

The bill got up to $9,000, the amount I had written checks for. I thought, "Gee, I better find out how I'm going to pay this back." Mr.

Brooks went right along with me. The first day I came back down to the bank Mr. Kirby was sitting in his big chair looking out the front window. He didn't look at me at all. He knew what had happened. Kirby lived in the big house on the corner of lower side of Julian Street. The upper side was the one Burdick built. He's the one that put up the money for the handle factory.

We had plenty of help all along, that's for sure. We moved some of our things in the middle of December because the downstairs was finished enough to live in. The plumbing wasn't done yet. We started living in our new house January 1, 1941.

Wilma 1949

Wilma was still working at Scintilla. When the war started up, there was a bus she could ride to work, from Bainbridge to Sidney.

During the war Scintilla started getting government contracts. The government raised the wages so high nobody could compete with them. These contracts were cost-plus because it included higher wages; causing everything to be quite high. After the war was declared over, the contracts were not good anymore, so a lot of people were laid off.

Wilma continued to work at Scintilla through the war. Then she decided she'd rather stay down here in Bainbridge. In the Eastern Star there was a girl who lived in a room up on Bixby Street, from Whitney Point. She told Wilma she worked for Dr. Suplee in the lab. She said she couldn't work for Dr. Suplee any longer and was going to quit. Maybe Wilma could take that job. So she went down and got the job from Dr. Suplee in the lab.

Suplee started experimenting with milk and learned that milk had to be pasteurized. He also measured the vitamin content and other nutrients.

She worked there until he died and the lab was sold to Foster D. Snell of New York. They came and built the lab into what was nicknamed "The Rat Factory." She stayed there. Esther Clark was the head of the company here. Esther married Leo Smart and he thought he should run the company, and that didn't work. Esther decided to quit.

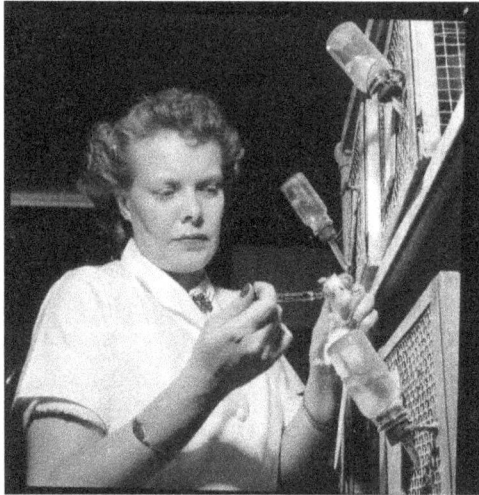

Wilma at the rat lab in 1952

A woman from New York came to run things and she didn't like the way it was run, all this work with rats. Wilma didn't get along with her. I told her to quit working there before they put her in one of those cages. She did and decided to stay home.

In about a week or so, towards Christmas time I came home one night and she said, "Roland Peckham has an add in the newspaper. He needed someone to work at the drugstore for the holidays."

She asked if it'd be all right if she started that job. I told her if she wanted to. She started that job at the drugstore working for Roland Peckham.

She stayed right there and when Jim Noyes and Roland Peckham went together, she went right along with it. Then Jim retired and Roland retired and they sold the business to Ernie Gestelli. She stayed there until I retired from the gas company when I reached the age of 65. Wilma retired too, but she didn't have any income. She wasn't old enough to draw Social Security.

As long as Hudson Lyon lived we paid him a certain amount monthly for the property where we built our house. When he died in 1950, my father was executor for his estate. Hudson had left everything to Cornell University and it was supposed to go towards their religious education program. I don't think it ever happened but that's what he wanted. All of a sudden, I was supposed to send the money to them, the amount that I owed Hudson. I had to borrow some more money so I could pay the balance to Cornell.

I had the deed to the property. Everything fell into place. It turned out fine with the bank; I had received $12,500 building the house, which was the mortgage. Then I borrowed money to send to Cornell.

When Hudson died I had a lot of work to do on his house. Hudson had done a lot for our family during his lifetime. The house was next door to us. He had tenants upstairs. Downstairs had to be redone. I had to redo the plumbing, rewire and do a lot in inside work there. He had a pipe less furnace and that's where he lived, right on top of that register.

I had to get rid of the furnace. It was an old furnace and used coal. Then he had an oil unit put in. I took it out as fast as I could and put in a new oil furnace with air ducts in the downstairs. The folks upstairs didn't want to be bothered. Finally the work was all done downstairs. I don't know how there was enough time to do all of this on my own with the work at the mill, but I did.

Wilma and I began many years of enjoying our new home. Wilma liked to cook. She had learned a lot of fancy cooking and liked to do new special dishes. She learned a lot from her mother who was Swedish. In school she was in the homemaking class and learned some things there.

Once she was in Albany going to school, she worked part-time in some restaurants. She learned the latest about fancy cooking. She always liked cooking and I was her guinea pig. Wilma would try a new recipe on me. I didn't mind, I'd eat anything that got in the way.

Frank and Wilma 1954

Wilma belonged to the Eastern Star. She got me into it and we attended many Easter Star meetings. Wilma would put on a Swedish smorgasbord for different occasions. It was a lot of work but that's what she wanted to do.

She did a lot of knitting and crocheting. She enjoyed knitting me sweaters like the one I'm wearing, and covers for our chairs and the sofa. Wilma made the tablecloth on dining room table and also made things for fundraisers that were sold to make money. I learned some from it because I had to help her a lot. She would do this work while she watched television. Sometimes she'd have to rip it up and do it over, but most of the time it turned out all right.

Wilma was always busy. We didn't have any children of our own, but we always had children here. If it wasn't our nieces and nephews, sometimes it was the neighbor's kids. Later on these children started growing up and we still enjoyed their visits.

One of the guys who worked for us at the mill, Russell Partrice, had a sister who lived down in South Carolina. They had an oyster business there and her husband died. She asked Russell if he'd come down and help her. They had lived outside Afton and had moved to South Carolina. They had a daughter who was here in school and she had a boyfriend. He lived up Bigsby Street. She wanted to stay here and finish school. She lived with us until she was out of school and then went south. Her boyfriend was Bud Andrews. He used to come here to visit with her. We had a record player that was a console with a radio in it. When young folks would come in, they'd play the records and visit.

We had our niece Ann, who was Olga's second daughter. She went to school in Masonville and when she finished grade school, she had to go to Sidney. She met Ron Marble up there. She didn't dare take him home because her father would kill him. Somehow they would get together and come here in the evenings, play records and visit. They married later on and now live in Florida, in her parent's house.

Wilma had a cousin, quite a bit younger. Her mother lived here and her father was in Washington, DC, working. She was in school where she met her boyfriend, Corkey Landry. Corkey's mother thought Wilma's cousin Violet wasn't good enough for her Corkey. Therefore, he couldn't bring her up to his house. So they would meet here in the evenings. There was always someone here and we enjoyed them. They weren't doing any harm. Violet went to a girl's school in Maryland, after her high school graduation. Corkey went into the Army Air Force, and they kept in touch with one another. They ended up getting married and went to Maine to live. Then when Corkey retired they went to Florida to live.

Wilma also made some of those crafts with plastics like coasters and stationary books to hold stamps, writing pad and pen. A lot of these crafts went to the Eastern Stars to help raise money and some to the church.

Wilma had joined the Eastern Star before we were married. Her mother, sister and she had joined the Eastern Star here in Bainbridge. Her father was already a Mason, so they could join the Eastern Star. She had started as a Gustafson. We were married May 28, 1938, so at the final degree she was a Doolittle.

In 1943 when I joined the Masons, she wanted to go through the chairs and be a matron. So in 1947 I was her Patron. In those days the Eastern Stars were the Mason's ladies. They had to have a Mason when they had a meeting. In 1949 she was appointed a District Deputy with the state. We did quite a lot of travelling to each Eastern Star in the district. There were 18 in this Chenango district. She had to take the message from the Grand Chapter in New York City around to each Eastern Star at night. That took a lot of time. We went to some meetings outside the district, too.

We went to Rochester a couple of times at night. One place was up at Old Forge and stayed all night there. That was before they had motels. They started having cabins, so we stayed in a cabin and ate in a restaurant.

Since we first joined the Eastern Star and Masons we've met a lot of people. In those organizations everyone is the same. A lot of them were people we wouldn't have met otherwise.

When Wilma's sister, Olga was in the Eastern Star and lived in Masonville, there was a guy there who had been a patron many times. He was the patron while Olga was matron. When the big district night came, which is when a large number of VIPs attend, the patron took sick that afternoon and couldn't come. The decision had to be made as to cancel the meeting. Finally Olga called Wilma to see if I could go over to be her Patron. Well, I had never worked with those women over there. No idea as to how they did their work there. Between Wilma and Olga, I volunteered. Now a days that would be illegal because it's a different district, I didn't belong to the Masons over there.

For that big meeting, I was Olga's Patron. We managed to get through it but it was a bit awkward; however it turned out all right. I guess there were people there who didn't know the difference. The guy who had been the patron over there, knew the ritual and went through it like a "house on fire". The only way you knew he was done was when he stopped. I didn't do it that way. We got a few comments but never heard any objections to what we did.

While Olga was Matron, we went over there a few times to visit when they had a meeting. Their meetings weren't the same as ours. Leonard, her husband, was not into that. He wasn't a Mason until later on.

We also belonged to a Pinochle club and met once a month. We had a regular meeting and then played Pinochle. We put in twenty-five cents apiece each time we played. Then in July we'd take that money and go somewhere for dinner. We had a vice president, president, secretary and treasurer. Also there were rules to go by. Most of the time we had three tables, four people at each table. We played the game and the winners of that table played the winners of the next table. This went all the way around. We had a time limit, when we had to stop. There was the meeting, then time for refreshments. The hostess had to provide refreshments when it was their turn to have pinochle. We took turns having it at each house.

Wilma and I were in this club for several years. Once we had 4 tables at our house, 2 tables in the living room, one in the dining room and one in the kitchen. Most of the time, it was just 3 tables.

Sometimes, one of the couples would have to move and we'd have to get someone else in their place. To keep the women from trying to out do one another, we had to have rules. It was pretty well organized.

There are only 2 of us left. Esther Hutchinson, just had her 95th birthday. The rest are long gone.

I joined the Masons in 1943. You had to work your way up through to the Master. I worked my way up through all the chairs and was a Master of 1954. I've been Master since at different times. I've always had an office in the Masons. Some of us went to Afton to join the Royal Arch Masons. That's the next step up. The Master Masons were three degrees, and joined the Royal Arch Masons for four more degrees.

You could work your way right on up to the top if you had money and time enough to the thirty-second degree. I didn't go any further as there were too many other things to get done. The mill was keeping me very busy.

Wilma and I started living in our new house January 1, 1941. We lived at 5 Kirby Street together for 65 years and I am still living there today.

Wilma died in 2006 at age 89.

Frank and Wilma's cabin at Brackett Lake 1979

Brackett Lake Cottage

My friend Jim Thorp had the first cottage there on Brackett Lake and Wilma and I went over there once in a while for a picnic or to visit. Jim and I liked to go fishing. This was after he married his second wife, Blanche. She and Wilma would get together for a visit and sometimes to prepare food.

My father and Jim Thorp had become friends many years ago. He owned the Bainbridge Garage when my father would go there with his car. His wife did a lot of work at the church. Sometimes I went with my father and got acquainted with him. My father, Jim and I would go hunting.

One day Jim told me the little cottage next door to them was for sale. The people who owned it hardly ever used it. Someone who lived in Oxford built the cottage and they sold it to the present owners. The property was grown up and neglected. You could hardly see the house for all the overgrown brush and trees.

I didn't have money to buy it. I thought maybe I'd borrow the money and fix it up, then sell it for a profit. I took the risk and bought it. Wilma didn't want any part of it. She wouldn't go near the cottage.

Once in a while I'd have a chance to go over there to work. I cleaned up outside and then inside. Finally the cottage was so it could be used. I thought maybe now I could sell it; get my money out of it.

One day I was going over to do some work inside and Wilma decided to go along. She had not been in there before. Wilma got to thinking maybe it would be nice after all. The cottage was ready enough so we could stay over night. When we were over to the Thorps to visit, then we stayed the night in our cottage.

At this time everyone had to go up to the "county seat" up at the edge of the woods, towards Oscar and Marian's place. It was a double outhouse, "His" and "Hers" and had a path going up to the woods to get there.

Well, it happened that Wilma needed to go in the night. She couldn't go through there in the middle of the night with all those wild beasts. I escorted her to the outhouse. This was a real drawback. Next we knew, I dug a hole and put in a septic tank. I put barrels in the back of the house for rainwater to use to flush the toilet. Also, a place for the toilet had to be built. We didn't have to go up to the "county seat" anymore. She got so she liked it over there and we used it quite a bit and decided not to sell the cottage after all.

It seemed I couldn't get much done at home on the weekend. People would come and want to get materials from the mill. So we decided to leave for Brackett Lake as soon as we closed the mill at noon on Saturdays. No one could reach us because the cottage did not have a telephone. It worked pretty well until a couple of people found me. That wasn't very often.

When I went to work for the gas company, I had to have a phone if we were over there. When I was on call, we had to be at a place where we could get calls. Therefore, I had to put in a phone.

We became acquainted with a couple from Tennessee who lived there next to us. The people who built there came up from Vestal, N.Y. He and his father came up. Their uncle had a sawmill in Green, and brought their materials from him to build a cabin. He and I worked together putting in a dock there on the lake. They had one son plus an adopted son, both about the same age. These 2 boys had a big time there at the lake. They had snorkels and were swimming around in the lake.

After about two years this family by the name of Jenks became so active in other activities such as their church and organized sports, that they couldn't spend much time there anymore. They then sold it to this couple from Tennessee. She was a professor at the University of Tennessee. They had a little farm outside of Knoxville. Most summers they'd come up here although she was gone most of the time. She went on tours with some of the students, sometimes to England and other countries.

Her husband stayed there in the summertime. Their cabin didn't have a toilet, so they used the outhouse. Finally, they did drill a well so they had water. Otherwise, they had to carry water from the pump down in the grove. Everybody could get water from there. We didn't because we weren't there much and could carry our water from home. There was always rainwater to use.

The Thorps put in one of those chemical toilets so they didn't have to go up to the "county seat" either. The man next door and his brother-in-law drilled a well and put in a flush toilet.

Before the couple from Tennessee came, the cabin was one big room, with a loft where the boys had slept. There were bunk beds up there. Downstairs the couple had a bed in the corner.

But when the Jenks came there, they partitioned off the bedroom, the kitchen and put in a gas stove in the kitchen. They had Olga's husband Leonard do some work for them while they were there. They wanted a stairway, so he built one to go upstairs. At this time there was no floor up there. Jokes were made about where did the stairway go? So the wife had Leonard do a lot of work. He put in the upstairs floor. They had a fireplace there since it was built, but they put in a gas wall furnace in the other end of the room.

That work was all completed and then Mr. Jenks died. She didn't want the cabin any longer and kept asking me to buy it. I told her I couldn't afford that. She kept asking until finally she got the house down to $16,000.00. I told her maybe that would work, if I could pay by the month. So she set it up that way and I made payments.

Now Wilma and I had 2 cottages on Brackett Lake. I had to do a lot of work on it to keep it so we could use it. It wasn't a camp anymore, and we couldn't rough it. Wilma had to have all the conveniences. First, we had to have hot water so I built a place on the back for a gas water heater. The house was very cozy and there was a nice view of the lake.

We had a front porch that we used quite often. I put plastic that I could roll up to close the porch in when it was cold and couldn't use it. There was a porch table attached by hinges along the inside, and when put up made a nice table. I made some benches for it. Maybe 10 people or so could sit along the table and they had a nice view of the lake. It worked well for picnicking.

Then the door where we went in was a nuisance to go there and unlock the door when it was raining. So I built a deck, and then the deck had to have a roof over it. That was very convenient. I placed my grill out there in front. Outside we also had a stove and a little fireplace where we could roast marshmallows with the kids. The stove we had at the other cottage and moved it over and had it set up for clambakes at our new cabin.

Sometimes we had the Eastern Star picnics there. After I was working at the gas company, we had the company picnics there as well. There was a lot of entertaining going on; family visits and reunions were pretty frequent in the summertime.

Eventually we put in carpet on the floor and a television. Our cabin was roughing it with the modern conveniences. Wilma really liked it there. I had to make a lot of adjustments because I went and married a "city kid."

Jim Thorp built rowboats and earlier he and some others had built some speedboats. There were some that he built kept at the grove. We had pine trees he could make boat sides out of.

So Jim says to me, "Why don't you build a boat?" I told him, "I don't have time to do that, and I don't know how."

Then he said, "If you'll furnish the trees for the sides, we'll build them down in my shop. We'll build two. One for the lake and one Wilma can have for the river."

Wilma tried the boat one time in 1936

That's what we did; we built two rowboats in our spare time. Jim didn't use the one here on the Susquehanna River and I didn't use the one on Brackett Lake. It's quite a hassle having a boat on the river, unless you left it there. I decided to take the boat over to the lake. Wilma liked being near the water but didn't want to get in the boat. I finally did get her into a rowboat one time.

One year the rowboat was in really bad shape. I had it fixed a few times and finally came a time that there was not much to fix anymore. That was when for our anniversary we went down to Binghamton and bought an aluminum boat. We brought it over and put it on the lake. I got her in it once. Otherwise, she didn't want anything to do with it.

Sometimes I would take people out in it when we had company, and take some of the boys fishing. That aluminum boat was used quite a bit on the lake.

As the years passed by we decided to sell our Brackett Lake cottage.

The Tex Gas Company

Newton Hovey had found out that I was going to sell the mill, and he wanted me to come to work for the Tex Gas Company. I said, "No, I don't think so." I hadn't had anything to do with anything such as that. But he kept at it until one Saturday he stopped by with an application form for me to fill out. He said, "I have a stack of them on my desk." I filled it out, and he called me the next morning, Sunday, and wanted me to go to work Monday morning. I told him I couldn't do that, as there were custom jobs that had been promised at the mill.

I wasn't too excited about going to work up there. Finally I got things caught up and went up to try it. I might not like it and he wouldn't either. I knew Newton Hovey since we were little kids and didn't know how that was going to work. Newton was kept on as head of the Sidney branch of Tex Gas. So at age 55, I went up to work there and tried it for 10 years.

This job was opposite of anything I had ever done. This was a whole new career. They hired me for a truck driver in 1968, but there's a lot more to it than just driving a truck. You have to know something about handling the product.

The folks I worked for were from the Union Texas Petroleum and their office was in Delmar. When I went to work there, they came right down to talk with me. They were taking over Fuel Lane Corporation, so I was the only one working for them, because the others were still working for Fuel Lane. I told them I didn't know anything about handling this product, and I've got to learn how. They said that would be all right. They would tell me when there'd be a class I could attend. They never said I had to. But they let me know about the classes.

I took 2 correspondence courses from the University of Texas and got a raise in pay. When I finished those, I received a certificate. The folks in the office wanted the certificate to put on the bulletin board to show what educated people they had working.

In two years I qualified to do anything that anyone else could do there. Most of it, I was more qualified because I had recent education, whether it meant anything or not. I had to learn pretty quickly how to handle the gas before getting into trouble. I never did get into any trouble but there were a lot of places for it.

The company moved their office to Albany. There were 3 bosses there and they'd come down to see how things were. They asked if everything was all right.

I'd say, "Things are good." This work was probably the best thing I ever did because I had the benefits, and a good paycheck. At that time, they paid $5.00 an hour. That was good pay then. The minimum wage was $3.25. I had a lot of overtime. It wasn't very long and I was getting $7.50 an hour instead of $5.00. This was the best thing I had ever done.

I was hired as a truck driver and contractor and could do service work. It was interesting to me. They paid my hospital insurance and gave me a pension. I retired in June at the age of 65. They continue to pay my insurance at 80% and I pay 20% since my retirement. The company policy was you had to retire when you were 65. I was 65 so it was time to retire. That was Nov. 1, 1978.

The company did a lot of nice things for me. They bent over backward a lot. They sent a letter telling me about their policy in June. One day I was hauling gas to a commercial company, F. M. Burt, in Oneonta. The company asked me to unload and then go by the Social Security office. They were expecting me that day and let me get my social security started. They let me work until November 1 as my birthday was in October.

The Tex Gas Company had a retirement party for me. They presented a story to me about the "Little Old Ladies" on my route. When going from door to door on my route, some of these ladies would come to the door with their nightgowns on. One morning the company had a breakfast for the employees in a restaurant above Sidney and we were allowed to bring our wives. So I brought Wilma to the breakfast.

There was a waitress taking care of us there, and one of the fellows at the breakfast told Wilma that she was one of his "little old ladies." They told the story about the little old ladies on my route and presented a little doll to me at the retirement party, and called it the "Little Old Lady."

Frank apparently was a trusted employee who often might encounter some dangerous assignments according to this story told by Gary Darling, the Bainbridge Town and Village Historian. "I enjoy hearing the story of Frank being a link in the chain of men and machines that kept the railroad running efficiently through the area. At the time he was working in the gas industry the railroad had frequent 'passing tracks' where trains could pull in and wait for an opposing train to pass. The switches were operated by remote control from a central dispatch office near Albany. Winter was an enemy and switch heaters were required to assure proper operation when there was snow and ice. Frank was the man who kept the gas tanks filled so the trains could keep running. Whenever possible the switches were located at a road crossing where the tanks could easily be filled from the truck. This was not always possible so he would have to drive his truck a considerable distance along a railroad service road adjacent to the track. In these cases he had to meet a railroad employee who would go with him and call the dispatcher to assure that no train would pass the spot while Frank was there servicing the tank."

Our house at 1020 Tennessee Avenue, St. Cloud, Florida.

The Snowbird Years

Wilma's folks decided they couldn't stay in New York another winter and moved to Florida. They went down to see what it was like. The Gustavsons met some people there. One of them was a real estate person who had worked with Wilma's father, Verner, here in New York. He would buy up some estates; sell the property, by selling it off in auctions. He worked in real estate, too, with this man, and they decided to buy some land in Florida.

Verner started building houses where they were, in St. Cloud. That's how we happened to go down as well. He built the house we lived in, on Tennessee Avenue. It was built for another couple, and when the time came for the couple to take the house, they didn't want it. So Wilma's father took it over.

After Wilma's mother died in 1970, Verner wanted us to buy his house. We got a big break on it. We went to the lawyer and got everything straight, and bought the house in 1972.

Wilma and I liked to go to Florida on vacations in the winter as Wilma's family was there in St. Cloud. After we bought their property we began to rent it out until I retired in 1978. I had finally sold the mill and was able to buy this house but I was still working at the gas company here in New York.

There was a couple, a man and his wife who lived outside Cortland, that we became friends with in Florida. He had been going down in the winter and buying places that were rundown. Then he'd fix them up and sell them. That's what he did in the wintertime. When he couldn't do that anymore, he and his wife wanted to rent our place starting in 1972. They rented for two years. The people who lived across the road from Olga and Leonard in Masonville, NY, retired and went to Florida. This couple had decided to buy a lot and build a house on it. But they called us to ask if they could rent our Florida house. We let them and that's how we started going down.

The last winter they had it, they came back up north and put their house on the market. They had made arrangements to have a house built on their lot; to be in there by the next winter but things didn't work out that way.

The summer came, and they wanted to rent our house again and in the summertime, too. Their house here had been sold and they had to move while their house was being built.

In 1978, the first of November, they were in our house and it was getting towards mid-December. We were getting ready to go down. I had retired from the gas company, and they were still in our house. They said they thought their house would be so they could live in it. It turned out that the day we arrived was the day they moved out.

Both of those families who rented our house treated the house as if it were their own. All we had to do was walk in.

In the meantime, I had bought an empty lot next to our house. No one could build next to our house. We had quite a little property there.

From that day on, we spent every winter there. We usually left to go South after election day in November and returned to Bainbridge in April in time to file our taxes.

We became involved in a lot of things there in St. Cloud. One group we were a part of was working to raised money to build some apartments. We worked putting on dinners and fundraisers.

There was bingo once a week where I was calling the numbers and Wilma and the ladies collected the money. We had a lot of fun doing that.

We also joined the New York and New Jersey Club that met once a month. The first thing I knew they made me Vice-President for a couple of years. Then they elected me President for 10 years and appointed as member of the Board of Directors for 18 years. It was a lot of fun running that club. These were mostly people from this area of New York State. This club raised money for a children's home outside of St. Cloud. We had to pay rent in the senior center where we met, and also to find some entertainment that charged a fee.

That worked pretty well until the city started their meal program. Before this, some liked to come in early to play cards before our potluck meals, then the meeting to decide what we were going to do. We always raised money to donate.

Wilma and I were also in a church group that met once a month, who had a dinner and program. This was the Presbyterian Church in St. Cloud. It was bigger than the Presbyterian Church in Bainbridge. They had about 500 members. We were honorary members, because we didn't live there year round. Our membership stayed in the Bainbridge church. This St. Cloud church printed a photo directory and we were a part of that book, with our picture, names and phone number. This was the same church Wilma's parents were a part of.

We enjoyed our winters in St. Cloud, Florida. 1989

We joined a group called Retirement Home Auxiliary, in St. Cloud, Florida, which was raising money to build apartments like here on South Main. We put on dinners, played Bingo once a week, and finally got enough to buy some land. The board of this group ran the Community House for the city. We worked with federal and local grants, and large donations to build a multimillion-dollar shelter for the city of St. Cloud.

We were getting ready to build but wouldn't furnish sewer and water. So we had to find another piece of land, which we did, and built 30 units with a clubhouse. The government began to get their hand in the project so the group began to get smaller, and that's when we opted out of it, too. Several years ago, in 2006, a developer bought it from the group.

We went down every winter until 2007. This was after Wilma died.

My garden on Kirby Street. Nephew Charles and wife Melanie Sheldon pay a visit with their daughter Jessica in 1996.

Always a Garden

In preparing my garden each year it had to be plowed to get it in shape. Then I marked it out by the rows and planted the seeds.

First the weeds start coming up, and you have to take care of them. Pulling the weeds by hand was a lot of work. Harry Case was the 4-H agent of Chenango County. He came around to check all the 4-H gardens and projects. Later I had a calf that was 4-H. This was during my high school years. Most everything was done by hand.

Up on the farm before I was married, we raised potatoes so we would have potatoes year round. I had a half-acre of potatoes that I grew to sell and to use. I only did this one-year because I got mixed up with a "city kid" and had to make a few adjustments. So I had dug up a little place in Sidney around the mill to have a small garden. I had this maybe 3 or 4 years.

In the meantime, we had to move from Twin Rivers Inn, when they sold it, to the little cottage above town. From there we moved to Sidney into the duplex. During this time I still had the little patch of garden at the mill.

Then in 1940 we had never planned to have a house, but we had our house on Kirby Street. There was plenty of space behind it for a garden, including the land behind Hudson Lyon's house next door. It was a good-sized garden. When Hudson died in 1950, I lost that part of the garden. So I plowed up a place at the mill where we used to store lumber. That was a big garden down there. I had that garden until the mill was sold. I still had this little garden behind the house up until last year 2014.

I started using a rotor tiller after starting a garden at the mill. I still have the tiller, but not here. The last I knew it was over at Buntings Garage. Paul Sheldon and Mr. Bunting have both used it. The last three years, I couldn't use the tiller anymore. Paul has used it to help me.

The earlier gardens were all done by hand with a hoe. I used the old type push rotor lawn mower to cut the grass for a path to the garden. A lot of the equipment on the farm was run by hand or "boy power". Some things had a crank but we didn't have much machine power.

The earliest we planted was mostly in June. Even sometimes in June we've had frost. Our crops were separate from the garden. On the farm we usually had a couple acres potatoes, and the same with cabbage. Sometimes we had five acres or so of buckwheat. The buckwheat was made into flour for our pancakes, that we had every morning. One year we had five or six acres of oats and peas. Some of these were raised to put into the feed for the cows. We always raised corn, about ten to fifteen acres for the horses, chickens and pigs. The rest of it was grass for the hay.

When we had to store the cabbage, there was a place in back of the house near the edge of the woods where we chopped the cabbage trimmings and covered it with leaves. One year we did take the trimmings and fed them to the cows a little bit at a time, because it affected their milk. Before that, we had hauled the cabbage down and loaded it onto railroad cars on the track.

Sometime in January my Uncle Dan and family came up on Sunday for dinner and my mother had cabbage. He wanted to know where she got it, "down in the woods?" After dinner they took him down there and dug out a cabbage and looked at it. It was a little hard but he took it.

It wasn't long that we heard from him. He had a little grocery truck that he delivered in. He asked if he could come and get a load. That's where that cabbage went. He had a little grocery store where he sold produce. A produce guy came in and wanted to know where he had gotten the cabbage. Uncle Dan wouldn't tell him but told him he thought he could get some for him and that took care of the whole crop. I don't know how much we got for it but probably was a lot more than we ever had earned before.

In the spring there was a patch where we planted the cabbage seeds and had our own plants. Other people would come and get plants, too. When we planted the cabbage we had a pail we carried the plants in and the water. We dropped the plant and some water and the next guy came along with a hoe and covered them. That's the way they were planted.

When I had the big garden at the house, I raised sweet corn, beets, carrots, potatoes and tomatoes. One year I tried some watermelon down at the mill. Always I had tomatoes, radishes, lettuce, parsnips and rhubarb.

It's been three years since I've planted a garden. But I still put in tomatoes and potatoes. Usually, Wilma and I had enough potatoes to carry us through until the spring. When we went to Florida, we'd take enough potatoes to last while we were there.

Mabel, and her brothers Mark, Perry and Floyd Doolittle

Together with My Family

My mother's youngest brother was Floyd. I was his favorite. We went to Sidney quite a bit to see him. I don't remember him much except the stories I've heard. My uncle in Sidney said he'd like having me as a son because all he had were girls. One time we were there, and they had company for dinner. He put me right on top of the dinner table and had me walk along there. He was a barber in Sidney, and in later years a postmaster.

My mother's oldest brother Perry Doolittle and his family were closest to us. His son Andress "Andy" and his children spent a lot of time together with us. It was my Uncle Perry who had come up to the mill to work when my father's health kept him from a full day's work.

My cousin Andy and I got into a lot of trouble together. There were chores to do on the farm, and we always were trying to help. My Uncle Perry had a cider mill, and in the fall we had to pick up apples and make them into cider. Andy and I thought that after they squeezed the juice out and had the pumice, we could give the rest to the cows. We were helping by taking a load down to give to the cows. We didn't know that the cows couldn't have this. My uncle saw what was happening, and the cows were lying down and some were blowing up like balloons. We had lost some of them, and it was a very bad situation. That was one of the capers we got into and we learned not give extra food to the cows anymore.

Cousin and sibling playmates, L to R, Paul, Ellen, Dick, Andy, Joe, Frank, Ruth (all Doolittles) and Louise Morey, whose mother was a Doolittle 1922

Another time, Andy was up to my place. We both had bicycles and one of them had to have something done to it. We went into town to the bicycle shop for the repair and then decided to see a movie. It was pouring down rain when we came out. My mother had said if it rained to find a place to get out of the rain. Well, we went to Uncle Will's house to wait. Aunt Aliph had us take our clothes off and go to bed. Uncle Will lived on top of Kirby Street and was my mother's uncle.

My folks looked for us and saw our bicycles on Uncle Will's back porch. Aunt Aliph didn't tell Uncle Will that we were there. She got up early and had our clothes dried. She got us out of the house and headed for home before Uncle Will got up. We had some explaining to do when we got home. That was another caper we got into.

Uncle Will and Aunt Aliph at home in Bainbridge.

My father's sister Aunt Anna married a man in Binghamton, Daniel Transue. He had a grocery store there. They had me come down for a week in the summer to help out while their other helper took his summer vacation. This was a nice change for me and I looked forward to it each summer.

Aunt Anna Doolittle Transue

Our family doctor was Dr. Danforth, who was also on the Board of Health for Chenango County. He was treating my father's medical problem until he became so sick that my mother insisted he go to another doctor in 1950. He then went to Dr. Ralph H. Loomis in Sidney. By the time he operated on my father, it was too late and they just made my father comfortable from then on out. He died of cancer in 1956.

My sister Ruth Doolittle had a ruptured appendix and had to be rushed to the hospital. Dr. Danforth had been treating her before the rupture and had not expected this serious condition. Despite this Ruth survived and lived to deliver six healthy children and enjoy her retirement for many years.

I had scarlet fever and measles together, and Dr. Danforth treated me. He gave me strong medicine. Soon after this treatment, I started wearing glasses and my teeth started going to pieces. They claimed it had to do with the medicine I had to take. Dr. Johnson was my dentist and he had to pull my teeth.

Wilma and my doctor in town was Dr. Dodge, a good doctor.

I was the oldest of 3 brothers and 1 sister. My mother had me go to the library to get books to read to my brothers, Paul and Richard. But it seemed I was always working on the farm and they weren't. In later years that changed; as they became teenagers, they went to work on other farms so they'd get paid.

Siblings Frank, Richard, Ruth and Paul Doolittle 1920

My brother Paul went into the service in the Army and was sent to Australia and the Pacific for 5 years. When Paul got back, he married Marie Sheldon, and they lived in Norwich, N.Y. He became ill with malaria while in the Pacific during the war. Paul liked working in a garage on cars but he couldn't work a full week at a time there in Norwich because of the malaria. His doctor told him he'd have to go to another climate. So they moved to California where they retired. Paul died in 2004.

Richard went into the Army and was sent to Africa and then to Italy, during the World War II. He married Margaret Stevens before he went, and they had a daughter, Donna, while he was away in the war. She was 3 years old before he saw her.

When Richard got back, he wanted to work on a farm. His wife was against that, so he began working 2 jobs and sometimes 3 to get money together so he could work on the farm. My father fixed it so he could take over the farm. That's the way it is now, Richard has worked and owns the farm on Lyon Road. He is still living today and is 98 years old.

My sister Ruth had married about the time I got married, about 1939. They started a family and moved from one farm to another and finally settled on their own farm in Newton Hollow. Her husband Albert Sheldon died January 1947, and they had 5 young children, one just born. All were under the age of 10. They were farmed out for a few months and she took a job at Scintilla in Sidney. She got on her feet again and took her children, Fred, Fern, Charles, Paul and David back home again.

Ruth married again in a few years to Robert Hendrickson, who made a good home for the family. The children resented his discipline at first, but later realized how much he had done to help them. All those nieces and nephews were almost like our own children. Of course, nowadays, they are looking after me a little bit. We didn't have any children of our own, but if we'd had any, I don't think we'd have done any better than these nieces and nephews. Ruth and Robert retired in Florida and she died in 1996.

Siblings Ruth, Richard, Frank and Paul 1995

A few years ago I had a very bad case of arthritis and was unable to walk up and down stairs, or to stay on my feet. My niece, Donna Brown who lives in Tully, New York, came to my house as I had a doctor appointment. Her father is my brother Dick. She took me to the doctor because I was having trouble with my legs. The doctor sent me across the street for x-rays at the hospital. He said I had fallen and there was going to be fractures. They got the x-rays and took all they could think to take. No fractures were found. The doctor said I couldn't go home;

I'd have to go to a nursing home. Donna said, "No, he's not going to. He's going to live at my house." And that's what happened. She took me right to her house.

After all the x-rays and other tests taken in Sidney, then down to Lord's Hospital in Binghamton, over approximately 6 weeks. They finally decided I had arthritis in my lower spine. They said they could fix that with surgery. I said, "You've done enough research there and you're not going to do any surgery on my back until I find out more about it." That was the end of that.

We went back to Donna's and in a day or two I had a pain in my shoulder. It happens some when moving around. They thought it was a heart attack. So they got me into an ambulance and took me to the hospital in Syracuse. I was in there 3 days and they did all the tests for detecting a heart attack and no heart attack.

They decided to take me down to their physical therapy to find out what I could do and what I couldn't do. They thought I could go back to Donna's and made arrangements for the therapists to come out. One therapist came Monday, Wednesday and Friday. The other one came Tuesday and Thursday to Donna's house.

They had put me in a wheel chair. Well, they got me out of the wheel chair and on to a walker. Finally, they got me onto my cane. But in order to allow me to go home, to live by myself, I had to show them that I could get along all right. So I had to do things there at Donna's to show them I could do things at home. I was there maybe 10 weeks. I recommend Donna's Nursing Home!

If I had gotten into that therapy program first thing, I probably wouldn't have needed to go anywhere. It was pretty easy living at Donna's. To give that up to go home to do things for myself, was a little disappointing. But the neighbors, the Masons and other friends have all been looking after me. The Buntings across the street, Doriane and Paul, are very caring neighbors. They give me rides to church, shopping and to the doctor's appointments. Sharon and David my nephew help me quite often with different chores, too. I feel like there's always someone there to help me.

I was able to come home again and to walk up and down stairs. My washer and dryer are downstairs in the basement as well as my gas furnace and a wood-burning heater, so it was very important for me to regain my stability.

Now I use the exercise cycle for my arms and legs every morning while my coffee is brewing. It is making a big difference and I want to continue to walk.

Uncle Mark Doolittle's restaurant in Binghamton, 1910. Mark is holding his daughter Inez, and his wife Clara is standing second from the right.

Historical Topics

The first time I traveled on a train was when we lived in Ithaca, NY, when I was a young child. My mother brought me to Binghamton because she had a brother who had a restaurant there. Mark Doolittle and wife Clara owned the White House Dining Room in downtown Binghamton.

Mother's brother Uncle Perry Doolittle was father of my good friend and cousin Andy. He worked in a sawmill and farmed in the Bainbridge area and helped the family many times.

When we moved to the farm on Lyon Road, there were 23 people on our telephone line. It was hanging on the wall and everyone had a certain ring: so many short and long rings put together in a pattern for each customer. People would listen into others' phone calls, called party lines. We had to pay if we had to go out of our line, to call up over to central lines. We didn't get electricity until 1937.

We heard the early airplanes fly over our farm and everyone would run outside to see them. Clayton Weltch was the pilot for Scintilla. I got acquainted with him and his wife. He took me out for a ride, my first airplane ride.

The first President I remember was Herbert Hoover. The first election I voted in was 1930, I believe.

I got my first driver's license in 1929, and got a chauffeur's license in 1930. Mr. Burdick, a partner in the Mill, had a big LaSalle car. I was driving for him, and he had me take Edsen Colman back home to Syracuse in the LaSalle.

Edsen's father worked for the music store there. He had a battery operated RCA Stromburg –Carlson radio, and it had a long cabinet. It had all kinds of gadgets on it, speakers, headphones, and a gooseneck speaker.

He had 2 of them. They had A, B, and C batteries that were to be stored in the cabinet beneath the radio. It was probably about a 1928 radio. The electric radios had come out, so in Syracuse they couldn't sell the battery radios; therefore, he brought it home.

He asked me if I wanted it. I told him I couldn't afford that. He said, "Well, it's yours if you'll take it."

He wanted to get rid of it because it took up a lot of room and he had a small place. We lived in a fairly large farmhouse, so I decided to take it home and set it up in the living room. One of the speakers I put on the top of my mother's cabinet in the kitchen. We could hear all the speakers at once. I suppose that's stereo. That's the radio that we had and enjoyed for a while.

The first movie I went to the theater to see was downtown. Andy and I had the 10 or 15 cents that it cost, so we decided to see a movie.

I remember the Charles Lindbergh flight of 1927 and thought that was really something. He made a solo flight across the Atlantic from New York to Paris. I got his first book he published a few months later in 1927 about flying, called "We" and liked reading his story.

Prohibition was a problem, I suppose. It didn't bother me. There was one-year when cider caused a problem on the farm. My father had a corn harvester, and we'd go around helping neighbors cut corn and filling silos. George Strong, Harriet's father, was one person we helped. Most farms had cider and when it cured a little bit it became hard cider with a high level of alcohol.

They sent George to the field to give the workers some cider while they were cutting the corn. Someone came up to the wagon to ask about the cider so they looked for George. They found him in a ditch of bushes, curled up with that jug of cider.

Our family was interested some in sports. My father played baseball. They had a team over at Brackett Lake and one in West Bainbridge for a lot of years. These teams played back and forth. I remember going there in a buggy at a big oak tree at Brackett Lake. They had me as a mascot. When I was big enough, I played with them. We didn't have any connection to the Major League Baseball or anything. They were farmers who played for fun, on Saturday afternoons maybe twice or 3 times during the summer.

Jesse Doolittle played baseball in 1920's

The West Bainbridge field was down on the flat where the driving range is today, in back of the schoolhouse. The schoolhouse stood pretty much where the range is today. They had the outhouse of the schoolhouse to use. This school was demolished when they centralized. The spectators could sit up on the bank to watch the games. The Brackett Lake ball field was on the left as you drive in to visit the lake.

When the schoolhouse wasn't used anymore, the property went back to the former owners, in this case, the Baptist Church. The building itself was moved up near the Welcome Inn and it was added on to make a house. I think the year was about 1933. 1934 was the first school year, and they had to build on the Bainbridge school as children were brought in from all around.

Around the time of the stock market crash of 1929, there were some people like Harvey Wood, who had an insurance business and a feed store in Bainbridge. He and others would go to Florida to invest money in small pieces of land. Florida was having a boom down there selling land cheap to people around the town of Bainbridge. They gave their money to Harvey to invest in some lots, and he bought the parcels of land for them. Later they began to realize that the land was mostly either under water or swamp land. When they found out where it was, they had an awful time and blamed Harvey for losing their money. The land was no good and the money was gone.

When the Great Depression 1929-1939 came, it did not impact us. We really didn't know what was happening because we lived on the farm. It was bad times in other places, but we had plenty to eat. In the early 1930's I was working in the mill. A lot of people didn't have any work. I was working a 50-hour week and got $16.80 for the week. That was a lot of money back then. People were working in Scintilla shorter hours but getting about the same pay as I was.

Different things that President Franklin Roosevelt started up affected the workers, such as beginning to take deductions out of their paychecks. This was called social security and the Federal income tax. FDR signed the Social Security Act in 1935. Taxes were collected for the first time in the same year. We knew we couldn't spend any money we didn't have. President Roosevelt started programs to get people to work. People have to work in order to have money to spend. If one can't spend any more, then business suffers. I was fortunate to have a part-time job after school and to have the farm to provide for the family.

Frank earned his license to fly for Civil Air Patrol in 1944

In the first of the 1940s I had lived in Sidney where I had to register for the draft. I was in the Walton District and they called me up for being in Class One draft. I had to go for a physical and then I was Class One A again. When I had been called in about three times by 1943, I happened to mention it to Bob Felske. I just became acquainted with him. He said, "Why don't you sign up for Civil Air Patrol? They need some more men up there." So I signed up for the Civil Air Patrol. I got into that, and they never called me up again for the draft. Of course, Civil Air Patrol was part of the Army, and at that time it was the Army Air Force. The CAP was established Dec. 1, 1943.

Of course, I was home all the time that was most of the time. Our base was Mitchell Field in Brooklyn, New York but we didn't have to go there. Most of our orders came from Syracuse. Col. Grueller was over our squadron in Binghamton.

I flew the Army Grasshopper, a small trainer and most had one seat. It had no radio or anything that could be detected because the Germans had a lot of spyware. We used it because it could fly low, and didn't make a lot of noise. The Civil Air Patrols got a lot the information they needed by flying out over the ocean and spotting German submarines By calling back in their location they could give it to others to go out and take care of them. The Civil Air Patrol could do that and hardly ever got caught at it. There were no anti-aircraft shooting but some of the planes came back with holes in them. We used to call the plane "the bag with a motor on it." That's how I got into flying.

I don't know whether you have heard of him or not. In later years he used to come and talk to groups of seniors at their dinners in Bainbridge. He was at that time retired. We used to escort Grueller when he talked to the seniors, but Col. Grueller used to come to Sidney to check on us.

Frank Doolittle, its your plane now! - 2000

Frank flies again in 2000

I knew Col. Grueller when he bought a farm up on Rt. 235 out of Harpursville and Nineveh. The government I'm sure paid for that farm about three times because they put in an airstrip up there for him. He had Army Grasshoppers, Jeeps, and one Army duck there. That was an amphibious landing rig. Later on they improved the other part of the farm where they drilled. So the Army came in there to drill. Today some of the Boy Scouts go there to do their camping.

Going back to 1954 when I was Master of the Masonic Lodge, we had done things for the Boy Scouts, Troop 252, before 1954. But at this time they needed a sponsor, so we sponsored them and still do. All those years we've sponsored Troop 252. They have a scout house that was donated by Fred Lewis, the contractor. We have donated a lot to maintain the scout house over the years. A long time ago the scouts had a place for camping. Cameron Collins had a place up on Mount Pleasant where they could go and camp. They built a lean-to for a shelter. Cam got mad at one of the boys for something like marking the bark on a tree and so he had them move right off. They didn't know where they could go.

One of the boys was Orville Smith's son who lived in the next place above us. When he got home and told his father about it, his father said, "Move your stuff up on that piece of land, I think there's three acres of it." That was part of his farm. "Move your stuff right up there and don't worry about it."

So on a Saturday, the boys got everything ready to move and I took my big truck up there and moved them. They kept that piece of land. Well, three years ago they thought they had saw mill rights and considered the saw timber in there that they could sell. It needed to be cleaned out anyway.

We contacted this guy and he said he'd cut the timber out they could use and saw it into lumber. They figured it would furnish the lumber needed to build two new lean-tos. That was part of the deal, that he would take the timber out of there that he could use and saw some of it into lumber for the lean-to's, and deliver it. Do all of that. Also, they were to pile the brush up so it'd be neat. When they were finished, they had enough lumber for the two lean-tos and another building for a shelter. There was $800.00 besides that.

This was the land the boy scouts used for camping. We, the Masons, had taken the property over and got a deed for it not for Boy Scouts of America, but only for the Bainbridge Boy Scouts. It's a good thing we did that because now the council has taken over the scouts. They are having a hard time getting leaders, and I don't know how it's going to turn out.

The Bainbridge Scout House

There are a lot of regulations that have to be followed, making it hard for a volunteer leader who has a job to go to besides. The leaders now are required to take classes before they can be a leader. They have to take time off from work. I'm not sure what the future of the boy scouts will be. There are so many regulations now coming from the urban areas. The same thing is happening in a lot of organizations. This has also caused many of the Masonic Lodges to close up, because they want things run the same as in the city.

Our lodge is still going but our members are all getting old. The younger ones are not getting into things like the Masons and scouts. Lifestyles are different today. Now days the kids have everything planned for them.

In October of 1956, my dad passed away and was buried on his 70th birthday. He had cancer and before that, a heart attack.

My mother died in 1969 of a perforated bowel. I was out on the road when they contacted me. At the time she was living in an apartment up from us on Kirby Street. They took her to the hospital and she died after a couple of days.

My 100th birthday cake from my church family of the
First Presbyterian Church, Bainbridge, NY

A Case Study for Longevity

We all want to live a long life and Frank A. Doolittle is doing just that. From my observations and I've been told that his lifestyle involves habits that have helped him live over 10 decades. He has never smoked and never includes too much of anything. He balances his life with a diet of fruits, vegetables, and meats along with his daily exercises of climbing stairs and walking. He has a mini-cardio cycle he uses indoors for leg and arm exercises. This comes in handy during the cold icy winters in upstate New York.

Frank has been very happy to celebrate his 100th and 101st birthdays. He gets a lot of hugs and attention as well as many birthday cakes from friends, neighbors, the church family, cousins, nieces and nephews. The Lyon and Doolittle Reunion group gave him a cake and celebration for his 100th in 2013. Family and friends gather to celebrate his life and accomplishments more often now because these are wonderful days for Uncle Frank. We love hearing his stories of family and the history that has been his for so long now.

100th birthday family celebration dinner in Oneonta, NY. From L to R are Kim Sheldon Heath, Donna Doolittle Johnson Brown, Frank, David and Sharon Sheldon, Paul and Violet Sheldon 2013.

When Frank celebrated his 101st birthday, he wrote, "I've had another long birthday between church kids and church family, Mason Lodge, and a dinner at the Rt. 7 Café. The Buntings took me to the Old Mill for a nice dinner and I received about 30 cards and some phone calls. The Bainbridge Historical group had snacks and cards at the last meeting. I have lots of help from friends and neighbors." Anyone can see that he is happy to be around so many people that care about him.

First Presbyterian Church, Bainbridge has been
my church since I was a young boy.

Frank has recently been recognized as the oldest member of the First Presbyterian Church in Bainbridge. He was presented a certificate and embraced with accolades for his 80-year membership. Years ago two children adopted Frank and Wilma. They would sit with them while their parents sang in the choir. Since that time, Maya and Tanner Cliffe and their family have become an integral part of Frank's social life. The children's grandparents are the Bunting family that he speaks of so much. They are neighbors as well. Paul Cliffe, the father of the children faithfully takes Frank grocery shopping every Tuesday.

He is surely an inspiration to many young members who look up to him at church. It means a lot when there are many people who really seem to care for Frank.

The Masons recognized me for my 68-year membership. David and
Sharon Sheldon, Donna and Niles Brown were there for the occasion.

The Susquehanna Lodge of the Masons has recognized Frank for being
an active member for 68 years in 2013. This was quite an accomplishment
for Frank, because there are a lot of meetings and ceremonies to attend.
Because he no longer drives, someone picks him up once a week for the
Masonic meetings at Bob's Diner in downtown Bainbridge.

Frank Doolittle has lived through the Great Depression, the 2 World
Wars, the Korean War, the Vietnam Conflict, the assassination of President
Kennedy and the creation of social media. He recalls a childhood in
simpler times, which is all they knew back then. He often talks about the
10 decades of changes in the Bainbridge Historical Society meetings to
visitors who often come in to ask questions. When Frank stopped driving
he gave up his duty to open and tend the Grange Hall, which is where
the Bainbridge Historical Society has their collection and meetings. But
Frank is always available to answer questions when needed or tell stories
of Bainbridge history in person or over the telephone.

Gary Darling watches as I cut into my 100th birthday cake at
the celebration with the Bainbridge Historical Society.

The Bainbridge Town and Village Historian, Gary Darling, said
Frank "remembers town events, who the merchants were and items that
he purchased from them seventy or more years ago. When he gets on a
roll he can recite the relationships of many of the families in the West
Bainbridge – Union Valley area."

Gary goes on to say, "I cast a small shadow when compared to past
Town Historians like Hudson Lyon or Edward Danforth but I might not
cast a shadow at all if it were not for the guidance and counsel of Frank
Doolittle....He has a remarkable memory."

An enjoyable breakfast at Bob's Diner, Bainbridge

According to research "Eureka Alert", it is suggested that centenarians may possess additional longevity genes that help buffer them against harmful effects of an unhealthy lifestyle."[2]

Frank's family is happy to see him live so long because the same genetics he inherited may be passed on to them. He and Wilma didn't have any children of their own but the family will get some of the same genes through the family. These longevity genes help keep harmful effects from occurring. If a family member suspects he or she may have these good genes, it is probable to live a longer life if that member maintains a healthy lifestyle.[3]

---

[2] Albert Einstein College of Medicine at Yeshiva University, the study, "Eureka Alert."
[3] The Week, "How to Live a Long Life According to Science," by Eric Barker, Oct. 29, 2014.

The latest research goes on to say, "The average human lifespan keeps going up." Everyday we get older, but some of us age faster than others. We do have some control over how fast we age because of the choices we make.

Older people who have a positive outlook on aging lived 7.5 years longer, says Eric Barker. This research says stress isn't always a bad thing. We need some stress and the research showed that people who worked the "hardest live the longest."

I soon began to see a connection between more than 100 years of hard work to Frank's longevity. The study continues on to inform the reader, "Those who were successful, responsible and dedicated to things and people beyond them selves thrived in most every way."

Further research cites the importance of the things we can do to extend our life. These are having an important relationship with someone to talk with and share troubles. It's always good to associate with other healthy people. The study also indicated that a person who has the ability to love and to be loved is associated with longevity. They also list being a good person, such as giving help to others and receiving help.[4]

We are further told by the research in order to live a long life we must make ourselves happy. Some advice on improving one's happiness is to watch less TV, spend time with friends, increase levels of activity, help others and express gratitude for help from others and last and so important, to take on new challenges.

All the studies support the ideas of laughing and being happy, being optimistic, forgiving, staying out of debt, and getting enough sleep.

Another study connected a personality trait to longevity. This is conscientiousness. In a study of heart patients the more conscientious people were more likely to recover from a heart attack. They were better at taking their medications and more cooperative.[5]

Frank is determined to be as healthy and as strong as he possibly can be. He uses a lot of common sense, in making decisions. He will not take any chances of going outside if it's his mealtime or if the weather is cold and icy. Meals are always on a regular schedule at his house. He has his

---

[4] The Week, "Flourish: A Visionary New Understanding of Happiness and Well-being," Oct. 29, 2014, by Derek Isaacowitz.

[5] The Week, Terman Study, "The Longevity Project: Surprising Discoveries for Health and Long Life from the Landmark Eight-Decade Study", Oct. 29, 2014.

menu planned ahead of time and it must be well balanced with vegetables, fruits, a meat and bread. If you look in his refrigerator, there will likely be a casserole or other dish brought over by a friend or neighbor.

Frank said recently, "I worked hard all my life and I said you can't live that long, but I'm still here." As he smiles at that thought, you can tell that it's hard for him to visualize the countless number of happy and healthy years that he's been blessed with. He approaches his days with an eagerness and challenge that many younger than he is don't seem to have.

Our Uncle Frank was asked how he felt about living so long. He responded, "I feel guilty because I'm sure I've used up all my Social Security and other retirement benefits, so I must be taking someone else's."

When others asked him how he could remember so much so clearly about where everything was and who owned what, he answered, "Oh, it doesn't matter because there's no one left to challenge my memory." He is well known for his quiet sense of humor.

He and one other person, Julia Riley VanDenburgh, are survivors of his high school class of 1932. He misses all these friends of his generation. But he keeps a positive attitude, and keeps on enjoying activities he has developed over the years. Frank reads the newspapers daily and keeps up with all the current events.

The National Institute on Aging of the NIH recommends the following: As we age it's important to "stay active, because exercise is good for your health, strength, balance and flexibility." The NIA also cites the importance of nutrition. "Maintaining a healthy weight is important to your health," along with a well-balanced diet. They remind us to get active with a friend or family member, which is an excellent motivator.[6]

When the family goes into visit Uncle Frank at breakfast, he will be frying his egg, toasting his bread, slicing his fruit and sipping his juice and coffee. For lunch on a pop-in visit, he had 6 cooked baby carrots, a boiled potato, and a boiled onion in with his greens and a piece of meat brought in by a neighbor. He still loves his Mt. Dew on occasion. He makes every effort to have a balanced diet 3 times a day.

He has a lot of food brought in by neighbors and friends. Mrs. Baker from Baker's Maple Syrup in Bainbridge, and a member of the same church, bakes cookies and bring them by. When there are church picnics,

---

[6] National Institute on Aging at NIH, https:nccih.nih.gov/health/aging.

someone always goes by to pick up Frank. He enjoys the visiting and the food.

When this comment was made, "Uncle Frank, it's amazing how well you've done all these years," he answered, "It must be all that water I've been drinking all these years, from the lead pipe that brought the water from the natural spring to the house." The water flowed naturally into the cistern located in the basement.

Frank still manages to keep things going around his house there in Bainbridge. In a recent letter to a niece, He said, "I still do my laundry down in the cellar and all the necessary household chores like getting my meals, mopping and vacuuming." Frank lives on his own but has neighbors and friends who check on him, and ask him to accompany them to the grocery store.

"I stopped driving my car in June (2014) as I think my reflexes and vision are not like they used to be. I think I had driven long enough since my first driver's license was in 1929 and my chauffer's license in 1933. I had a classified license for driving gas trucks in 1968. In 1978 I went back to my regular driver's license. Now I am riding with other people."

Frank has been telling others, "I had to stop taking the old folks to the doctor." It was always a nice drive and visit for him when his 98-year-old brother Richard needed a ride to the doctor. It gave him an excellent reason to stop by the beautiful Doolittle family farm once again on Lyon Road, as well as helping his younger brother get to the doctor.

He makes sure he keeps his own regular doctor check-ups because he knows delaying the onset of diseases is very important to a long life.

A large part of longevity is hard work, something Frank has been accustomed with since childhood. Being the oldest sibling he found himself shouldering a lot of the work on the farm in order to get the chores done. With his father ill and his mother having many young children to tend, Frank did much of the work. In addition to the farm work, Frank always found afterschool jobs. He earned money to buy his first car and then gasoline to travel to school and work. These jobs gave him much of the confidence, skill, mutual respect and stamina needed throughout his long life.

Frank, our family centenarian gives credit to hard work and a loving family. Even while he might have been busy, he always gave those around him the courtesy and respect that was a part of him his whole life. The Bainbridge Town and Village Historian said he had known Frank Doolittle since a child coming in with his own father to the Trico Lumber Company to purchase small household repair items and shelving. Gary Darling said, "Even so, I was always treated with dignity and respect, receiving as much attention as the contractors who were buying by the truck load. Frank or one of the other employees would take me to the storage area and help me select the items I needed. Service must have been a very high priority item with the company."

One of my duties at my church is Greeter. I like
speaking with everyone at the door.

Now days we are overall healthier in our 60's and 70's than we were 100 years ago. Life expectancy now on the average is 78 years. Dr. Natalie Azar, NBC News medical contributor fills us in on some of the "factors contributing to the determination that 60 now represents middle age, including level of education, diet and lifestyle." She goes on to say, "60 is the new 40."

Frank Doolittle's life of 101 plus years is a study for our entire family to witness and it supports all the facts I could find on longevity. I will say with certainty that Frank is following all the rules for a long healthy life.

Frank's dedications to serve and lead were the same while living in Florida as they were in New York. He is always the same, no matter where he is.

As he signs his name to a family letter and his gratitude he writes a little note, "Thanks to all you folks do, to keep me informed."

At the end of his interviews for this book, Frank spoke right up and said, "I think we have pretty much covered everything."

Frank was interviewed from November 2008 to April 2015 on various occasions and was always intent on telling his story just the way it happened. We certainly want to thank Frank for that and pray that Frank stays with us many more years.

Lyon and Son, NY, 1909. Alton Briggs Lyon standing between the horse and dump wagon. Alton was son of George L. Lyon and Mira Doolittle Lyon.

Lyon Ancestry

There is a story told in our family about the four Lyon brothers William, Charles, Daniel, Samuel and a sister Clara Lyon (Seeley) who emigrated from Westchester, New York to Bainbridge, New York about 1803. The four brothers settled on farms adjoining each other that included a half section, about 320 acres, purchased by their father (Israel Jr.) for them. The father continued to hold the deed in this own name to insure against the sons divesting themselves of the land. The sister Clara, who married Harry Seeley, had her home three to four miles away, on the Susquehanna River, about one mile above Bainbridge village. The four brothers lived all their long lives upon the farms where they first settled and all reared large families: William 12, Charles 12, Daniel 5, and Samuel 13. The sister, Clara Seeley, continued in her home and reared 7 children. Descendants, more than one hundred years after their settlement, owned the four homes in 1906.[7]

The whole section in which these brothers settled was then a "howling wilderness" broken here and there by small clearings. There were some log huts of some daring pioneer left at these clearings. The old house is still standing in which Mr. and Mrs. Lyon went to keeping house but cooked their food the first warm weather, outside against a huge stump. Stones were gathered from the nearby fields for erecting a chimney. That house was 18 x 19 feet and was used to rear a family of 12 children.[8]

These earlier Lyon family members were buried on the homestead burial plot. The plot included graves of William and his family and of children and grandchildren. The plot was enclosed by a stonewall and was

---

[7] Lyon Memorial, page 207; Four Lyon Brothers, pages 4-5.
[8] Chenango Union, news article, "1872 Family Reunion", February 3, 1872.

well cared for by Horace Lyon and his son, Hudson H. Lyon and their families who inherited the homestead on Lyon Road. This family cemetery was next to the picnic shelter called Camp Sassafras. These graves and markers were all moved to West Bainbridge Cemetery during the 1940's.[9]

Our Uncle Frank tells a story that he was told as a child about these 4 brothers. He tells it this way:

The Lyon brothers who owned the farm where we lived had a brother who owned the next farm up. He also had the first place down in Newton Hollow. The brother who owned our farm wouldn't let him get across to go down there. So he had to go around by the road. The road was a turnpike. They charged him every time he went through the tollgate just to go from Lyon Road to Newton Hollow Road. The turnpike road was route 206. They didn't like that very well so one morning the one brother was going to have his son go down to the other farm and said, now if they charge you to go through the toll gate, you hook on to it with your team and fix it. So that's what he did. He took the gate down and part of the toll house with it and pulled it right out into the field. I expect there was more to it than that but that's the way the Lyons told it. This Lyon brother was believed to be Hudson Lyon's grandfather, the brother who wouldn't let the other brother go through.

It was a good many years later when Hudson wanted a marker to show where the tollbooth used to be. It took him a long time to go through the New York State Historical Marker department to get this approved as the first Toll Gate. Finally they made the sign and shipped it to Hudson. He got me to dig the hole and set it up.

The marker disappeared two different times and people wondered what had happened to it. The state occasionally picks it up, has it cleaned and painted. Then they put it back.

---

[9] Lyon Memorial, "Lyon Brothers of Bainbridge", page 152, and family knowledge of these graves moved to West Bainbridge Cemetery.

Hudson Lyon - cousin to Doolittles & Lyons - 1944

Hudson H. Lyon 1857-1950

Hudson Horace Lyon descended down through the Lyon brother Charles 1784-1879. Charles had 12 children, one of which was Horace Lyon, Hudson's father. Hudson went on to become the Bainbridge town historian and taught in one-room schools for many years. He and his sister Minnie lived on the family farm as his father aged and was no longer able to take care of farm.

This Lyon farm became the home place of Jesse and Mabel Doolittle when they bought it from Hudson Lyon in 1919, and Frank's brother Richard Doolittle lives there today. The farm has more recently been known as the Doolittle farm.

There is also a story told by Hudson Lyon about Samuel Lyon long before there was school centralization and the formation of a Bainbridge-Guilford School District. This takes place in the 1800's. The idea was to make the schools smaller and closer to home so the children did not have far to walk. These schools were the one-room variety and became a controversial issue. Sam Lyon thought the schoolhouse should be moved closer to his home because it was a long way for his offspring or relatives, one being Hudson Lyon, a nephew. He wanted one in Newton Hollow and decided to build a schoolhouse of his own after he was voted down at a school meeting to get the school closer. Hudson said it was nothing fancy.

The school needed a heater when it was time to open school so Samuel hitched his team of horses and went to the existing schoolhouse to take the stove. After an argument and there being a roaring fire in the wood burning stove, Samuel put a chain around the stove and yanked it out and off he returned to Newton Hollow with the heater. It was decided to move the original schoolhouse to another location and the new Newton Hollow school of Samuel Lyon was never used. [The Daily Star, Area schooling could be rough-and-tumble in 19th century, Oneonta, Mark Simonson].

Frank's cousin Hudson Lyon's grandfather was Charles Lyon (1784-1872) was one of the 4 Lyon brothers who settled in Bainbridge in 1805. Frank's second Great-Grandfather Samuel Lyon (1777-1855) was also one of those 4 brothers.[10]

The old house believed to be that of the Lyon brother, Charles, was still intact behind the Doolittle home on Lyon Road. It was moved and remodeled in the 1950s and now provides a home for John Doolittle, a son of Richard. Charles Lyon came with his parents when he was 5 years of age in 1803. His parents were William and Sarah (Wolsey) Lyon.

Probable original house of Charles Lyon family, one of 4 brothers who emigrated to Bainbridge, NY, in 1802.

---

[10] "Doolittle Family Tree Feb 9, 2007", sheldon187, ancestry.com

The Doolittle and Lyon
Family Tree

The marriage between Deborah Ann Lyon and Abel Stoddard Doolittle caused a big change in our ancestry tree. Our surnames have now mostly become Doolittle. In Frank's family there was a Doolittle who married a Doolittle, his mother and father.[11]

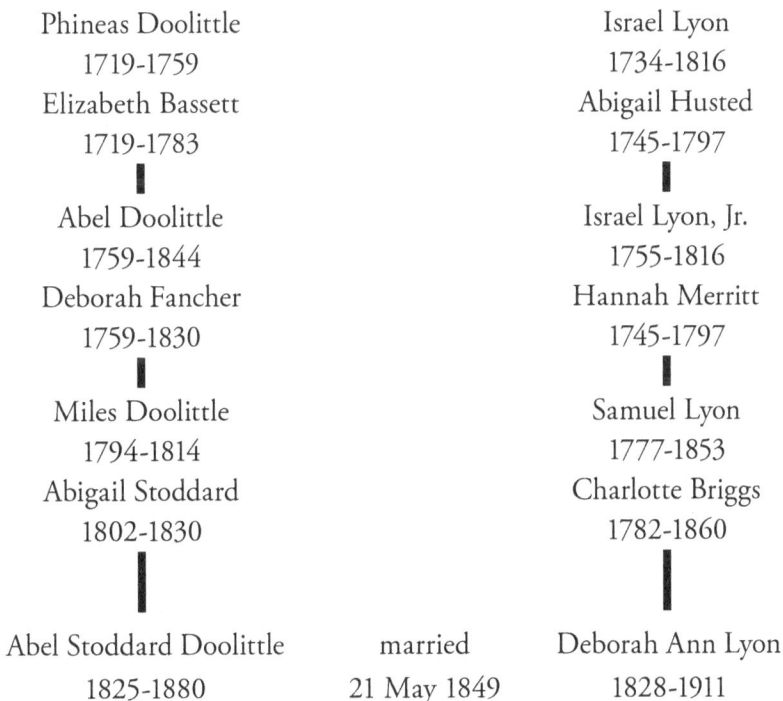

Phineas Doolittle	Israel Lyon
1719-1759	1734-1816
Elizabeth Bassett	Abigail Husted
1719-1783	1745-1797
❙	**❙**
Abel Doolittle	Israel Lyon, Jr.
1759-1844	1755-1816
Deborah Fancher	Hannah Merritt
1759-1830	1745-1797
❙	**❙**
Miles Doolittle	Samuel Lyon
1794-1814	1777-1853
Abigail Stoddard	Charlotte Briggs
1802-1830	1782-1860
❙	**❙**

Abel Stoddard Doolittle	married	Deborah Ann Lyon
1825-1880	21 May 1849	1828-1911

---

[11] "Flavius Hartsfield and Doolittle Family Tree", sheldon187, ancestry.com

Abel Stoddard Doolittle	married	Deborah Ann Lyon
1825-1880	1849	1828-1911

Their Children:

1. Arthur Miles Doolittle	1850-1927	m: Phebe J.Yale 1873
2. Albert Doolittle	1852	Did not survive.
3. Andress D. Doolittle	1854-1925	m: Cora B. Davis 1880
		m: Maude Wykes 1906
4. Alton H. Doolittle	1856-1875	Never married
5. Allen Doolittle	1856	Did not survive
6. Alice A. Doolittle	1858-1938	m: Allen Grannis 1877
		m: Newton Bartlow aft.1913
7. Almira Jane Doolittle	1860-1947	m: George L. Lyon 1879
8. Mary Abigail Doolittle	1863-1922	m: Sherwood Shapley1881
		m: Frank D. Morey 1899
9. Olive A. Doolittle	1870-1905	m: Arthur F. Earl 1890

Deborah Lyon Doolittle, center, and daughters, standing Olive A.
Doolittle Earl and Mary Doolittle Shapley Morey. Seated Mira Jane
Doolittle Lyon and Alice Doolittle Grannis Bartlow 1900.

| 1. Arthur M. Doolittle | married | Phebe Jane "Jennie" Yale |
| | 7 May 1873 | |

Their children:

| Anna Belle Doolittle | 1881-1969 | m: Daniel W. Transue |
| Jesse Richard Doolittle | 1886-1956 | m: Mabel E. Doolittle |

| 2. Albert Doolittle | 1852-1863 | Never married |

| 3. Andress D. Doolittle | married | Cora B. Davis |
| | 23 Dec 1880 | |

Their children:

Mabel Etta Doolittle	1882-1969	m: Jesse R. Doolittle
Perry Leland Doolittle	1884-1981	m: Mary Ellen Dwyer
Mark Arthur Doolittle	1887-1966	m: Clara L. Chauncey
Floyd Davis Doolittle	1888-1976	m: Marie A. Moscript

Note: Andress married Maude Wykes 20 May 1906
Their child: John Elliot (Doolittle) Hurlburt 1925-2009

| 4. Alton H. Doolittle | 1856-1875 | Never married |

| 5. Alice Antionette Doolittle | 1858-1938 | m: Allen E. Grannis |
| | 19 Feb. 1877 | |

Their children:

| Lina Bernice Grannis | 1883-1954 | m: Charles W. Swift Sr. |
| Orah Maude Grannis | 1887-1961 | m: Louis Alvah Wilder |

Note: Alice married James Newton Bartlow after 1913
No children from this marriage

| 6. Almira Jane Doolittle | 1860-1947 | m: George Leroy Lyon |
| | 24 Sept. 1879 | |

Their children:

Alton Briggs Lyon	1881-1916	m: Mina Anne Chauncey
Rena Mary Lyon	1887-1984	m: Sebert B. Hollenbeck

7. Mary Abigail Doolittle	1863-1922	m: Sherwood Shapely
	9 July 1881	

Their children:

Joseph Shapely	1880-1883	No marriage
Harold Blain Shapely	1884-1964	m: Elva Booth
Harrison Sherwood Shapely	1888-1918	m: Hazel Lyon

Mary Abigail Doolittle married Frank D. Morey 25 Dec.1899
Their children:

Zelda Marie Morey	*1903-1988*	*m: William C. Davey*
Myra Louise Morey	*1911-1975*	

8. Olive Anna Doolittle	1870-1905	m: Arthur F. Earl
	1890	

Their children:

Rexford Earl	1891-1892	No marriage
Shirley Marion Earl	1893-1913	No marriage
Stanley Earl	1895-1991	m: Mabel Clara Stone

Source:[12]

---

[12] "Flavius J Hartsfield and Doolittle Family Tree", sheldon187, ancestry.com.

Frank's Family, the Doolittles gathered on a porch ca.1914. Standing
L to R: Mark Doolittle, Marie Moscript Doolittle (Floyd's wife), Maude
Wykes Doolittle (Andress' wife), Mary Dwyer Doolittle (Perry's wife),
Jesse Doolittle, Clara Chauncey Doolittle (Mark's wife), Floyd Doolittle.
Seated: Perry Doolittle, Mabel Doolittle, and Andress Doolittle. Mabel is
holding Paul Doolittle, Andress is holding Joe Doolittle. Front row, L to
R: Frank Doolittle, Ellen Doolittle, Andy Doolittle and Inez Doolittle.

www.ingramcontent.com/pod-product-compliance
Lightning Source LLC
LaVergne TN
LVHW011333080426
835513LV00006B/325